The Hermits And Recluses Of The

Middle Ages

Edward L. Cutts

Kessinger Publishing's Rare Reprints

Thousands of Scarce and Hard-to-Find Books on These and other Subjects!

- Americana
- Ancient Mysteries
- Animals
- Anthropology
- Architecture
- Arts
- Astrology
- Bibliographies
- Biographies & Memoirs
- Body, Mind & Spirit
- Business & Investing
- Children & Young Adult
- Collectibles
- Comparative Religions
- Crafts & Hobbies
- Earth Sciences
- Education
- Ephemera
- Fiction
- Folklore
- Geography
- Health & Diet
- History
- Hobbies & Leisure
- Humor
- Illustrated Books
- Language & Culture
- Law
- Life Sciences

- Literature
- Medicine & Pharmacy
- Metaphysical
- Music
- Mystery & Crime
- Mythology
- Natural History
- Outdoor & Nature
- Philosophy
- Poetry
- Political Science
- Science
- Psychiatry & Psychology
- Reference
- Religion & Spiritualism
- Rhetoric
- Sacred Books
- Science Fiction
- Science & Technology
- Self-Help
- Social Sciences
- Symbolism
- Theatre & Drama
- Theology
- Travel & Explorations
- War & Military
- Women
- Yoga
- *Plus Much More!*

We kindly invite you to view our catalog list at:
http://www.kessinger.net

THE HERMITS AND RECLUSES OF THE MIDDLE AGES.

CHAPTER I.

THE HERMITS.

E have already related, in a former chapter (p. 3), that the ascetics who abandoned the stirring world of the Ægypto-Greek cities, and resorted to the Theban desert to lead a life of self-mortification and contemplation, frequently associated themselves into communities, and thus gave rise to the cœnobitical orders of Christendom. But there were others who still preferred the solitary life ; and they had their imitators in every age and country of the Christian world. We have not the same fulness of information respecting these solitaries that we have respecting the great orders of monks and friars ; but the scattered notices which remain of them, when brought together, form a very curious chapter in the history of human nature, well worthy of being written out in full. The business of the present paper, however, is not to write the whole chapter, but only to select that page of it which relates to the English solitaries, and to give as distinct a picture as we can of the part which the Hermits and Recluses played on the picturesque stage of the England of the Middle Ages.

We have to remember, at the outset, that it was not all who bore the name of Eremite who lived a solitary life. We have already had occasion to mention that Innocent IV., in the middle of the thirteenth century, found a number of small religious communities and solitaries, who were not in any of the recognised religious orders, and observed no authorised rule ; and that he enrolled them all into a new order, with the rule of St. Augustine, under the name of Eremiti Augustini. The new order took root, and flourished, and gave rise to a considerable number of large communities, very similar in every respect to the communities of friars of the three orders previously existing. The members of these new communities did not affect seclusion, but went about among the people, as the Dominicans, and Franciscans, and Carmelites did. The popular tongue seems to have divided the formal title of the new order, and to have applied the name of *Augustine*, or, popularly, *Austin Friars*, to these new communities of friars ; while it reserved the distinctive name of *Eremites*, or Hermits, for the religious, who, whether they lived absolutely alone, or in little aggregations of solitaries, still professed the old eremitical principle of seclusion from the world. These hermits may again be sub-divided into Hermits proper, and Recluses. The difference between them was this : that the hermit, though he professed a general seclusion from the world, yet, in fact, held communication with his fellow-men as freely as he pleased, and might go in and out of his hermitage as inclination prompted, or need required ; the recluse was understood to maintain a more strict abstinence from unnecessary intercourse with others, and had entered into a formal obligation not to go outside the doors of his hermitage. In the imperfect notices which we have of them, it is often impossible to deter-mine whether a particular individual was a hermit or a recluse ; but we incline to the opinion that of the male solitaries few had taken the vows of reclusion ; while the female solitaries appear to have been all recluses. So that, practically, the distinction almost amounts to this—that the male solitaries were hermits, and the females recluses.

Very much of what we have to say of the mediæval solitaries, of their abodes, and of their domestic economy, applies both to those who had, and to those who had not, made the further vow of reclusion. We shall, therefore, treat first of those points which are common to them, and then devote a further paper to those things which are peculiar to the recluses.

The popular idea of a hermit is that of a man who was either a half-crazed enthusiast, or a misanthrope—a kind of Christian Timon—who abandoned the abodes of men, and scooped out for himself a cave in the rocks, or built himself a rude hut in the forest; and lived there a half-savage life, clad in sackcloth or skins,* eating roots and wild fruits, and drinking of the neighbouring spring; visited occasionally by superstitious people, who gazed and listened in fear at the mystic ravings, or wild denunciations, of the gaunt and haggard prophet. This ideal has probably been derived from the traditional histories, once so popular,† of the early hermit-saints; and there may have been, perhaps, always an individual or two of whom this traditional picture was a more or less exaggerated representation. But the ordinary English hermit of the Middle Ages was a totally different type of man. He was a sober-minded and civilised person, who

* In the National Gallery is a painting by Fra Angelico, in which is a hermit clad in a dress woven of rushes or flags.

† "The Wonderful and Godly History of the Holy Fathers Hermits," is among Caxton's earliest-printed books. Piers Ploughman (" Vision ") speaks of—

" Anthony and Egidius and other holy fathers
Woneden in wilderness amonge wilde bestes
In spekes and in spelonkes, seldom spoke together.
Ac nobler Antony ne Egedy ne hermit of that time
Of lions ne of leopards no livelihood ne took,
But of fowles that fly, thus find men in books."
And again—
" In prayers and in penance putten them many,
All for love of our Lord liveden full strait,
In hope for to have heavenly blisse
As ancres and heremites that holden them in their cells
And coveten not in country to kairen [walk] about
For no likerous lifelihood, their liking to please."
And yet again—
" Ac ancres and heremites that eaten not but at nones
And no more ere morrow, mine almesse shall they have,
And of my cattle to keep them with, that have cloisters and churches,
Ac Robert Run-about shall nought have of mine."
Piers Ploughman's Vision.

dressed in a robe very much like the robes of the other religious orders ; lived in a comfortable little house of stone or timber ; often had estates, or a pension, for his maintenance, besides what charitable people were pleased to leave him in their wills, or to offer in their lifetime ; he lived on bread and meat, and beer and wine, and had a chaplain to say daily prayers for him, and a servant or two to wait upon him ; his hermitage was not always up in the lonely hills, or deep-buried in the shady forests—very often it was by the great high roads, and sometimes in the heart of great towns and cities.

This summary description is so utterly opposed to all the popular notions, that we shall take pains to fortify our assertions with sufficient proofs ; indeed, the whole subject is so little known that we shall illustrate it freely from all the sources at our command. And first, as it is one of our especial objects to furnish authorities for the pictorial representation of these old hermits, we shall inquire what kind of dress they did actually wear in place of the skins, or the sackcloth, with which the popular imagination has clothed them.

We should be inclined to assume *a priori* that the hermits would wear the habit prescribed by Papal authority for the Eremiti Augustini, which, according to Stevens, consisted of "a white garment, and a white scapular over it, when they are in the house ; but in the choir, and when they go abroad, they put on, over all, a sort of cowl and a large hood, both black, the hood round before, and hanging down to the waist in a point, being girt with a black leather thong." And in the rude woodcuts which adorn Caxton's "Vitas Patrum," or "Lives of the Hermits," we do find some of the religious men in a habit which looks like a gown, with the arms coming through slits, which may be intended to represent a scapular, and with hoods and cowls of the fashion described ; while others, in the same book, are in a loose gown, in shape more like that of a Benedictine. Again, in Albert Durer's "St. Christopher," as engraved by Mrs. Jameson, in her "Sacred and Legendary Art," p. 445, the hermit is represented in a frock and scapular, with a cowl and hood. But in the majority of the representations of hermits which we meet with in mediæval paintings and illuminated manuscripts, the costume consists of a frock, sometimes girded, sometimes **not,**

and over it an ample gown, like a cloak, with a hood; and in the cases where the colour of the robe is indicated, it is almost always indicated by a light brown tint.* It is not unlikely that there were varieties of costume among the hermits. Perhaps those who were attached to the monasteries of monks and friars, and who seem to have been usually admitted to the fraternity of the house,† may have worn the costume of the order to which they were attached; while priest-hermits serving chantries may have worn the usual costume of a secular priest. Bishop Poore, who died 1237, in his "Ancren Riewle," speaks of the fashion of the dress to be worn, at least by female recluses, as indifferent. Bilney, speaking especially of the recluses in his day, just before the Reformation, says, "their apparell is indifferent, so it be dissonant from the laity." In the woodcuts, from various sources, which illustrate this paper, the reader will see for himself how the hermits are represented by the mediæval artists, who had them constantly under their observation, and who at least tried their best to represent faithfully what they saw. The best and clearest illustration which we have been able to find of the usual costume in which the

St. Damasus, Hermit.

hermits are represented, we here give to the reader. It is from the figure of St. Damasus, one of the group in the fine picture of "St. Jerome," by

---

* Piers Ploughman ("Vision") describes himself at the beginning of the poem as assuming the habit of a hermit—

> "In a summer season when soft was the sun
> In habit as a hermit unholy of works,
> Went wild in this world, wonders to hear,
> All on a May morning on Malvern Hills," &c.

And at the beginning of the eighth part he says—

> "Thus robed in *russet* I roamed about
> All a summer season."

† For the custom of admitting to the fraternity of a religious house, see p. 66.

H

Cosimo Roselli (who lived from 1439 to 1506), now in the National Gallery. The hermit-saint wears a light-brown frock, and scapular, with no girdle, and, over all, a cloak and hood of the same colour, and his naked feet are protected by wooden clogs.

Other illustrations of hermits may be found in the early fourteenth century MS. Romances Additional 10,293 f. 335, and 10,294 f. 95. In the latter case there are two hermits in one hermitage ; also in Royal 16 G. vi. Illustrations of St. Anthony, which give authorities for hermit costume, and indications of what hermitages were, abound in the later MSS. ; for example, in King René's " Book of Hours " (Egerton 1,070), at f. 108, the hermit-saint is habited in a grey frock and black cloak with a T-cross on the breast ; he holds bell and book and staff in his hands. In Egerton 1,149, of the middle of the fifteenth century. In Add. 15,677, of the latter part of the fifteenth century, at f. 150, is St. Anthony in brown frock and narrow scapulary, with a grey cloak and hood and a red skull cap ; he holds a staff and book ; his hermitage, in the background, is a building like a little chapel with a bell-cot on the gable, within a grassy enclosure fenced with a low wattled fence. Add. 18,854, of date 1525 A.D., f. 146, represents St. Anthony in a blue-grey gown and hood, holding bell, rosary, and staff, entering his hermitage, a little building with a bell-cot on the gable.

A man could not take upon himself the character of a hermit at his own pleasure. It was a regular order of religion, into which a man could not enter without the consent of the bishop of the diocese, and into which he was admitted by a formal religious service. And just as bishops do not ordain men to holy orders until they have obtained a "title," a place in which to exercise their ministry, so bishops did not admit men to the order of Hermits until they had obtained a hermitage in which to exercise their vocation.

The form of the vow made by a hermit is here given, from the Institution Books of Norwich, lib. xiv. fo. 27a (" East Anglian," No. 9, p. 107). " I, John Fferys, nott maridd, promyt and avowe to God, oʳ Lady Sent Mary, and to all the seynts in heven, in the p'sence of you reverend fadre in God, Richard bishop of Norwich, the wowe of chastite, after the rule of sent paule the heremite. In the name of the fadre, sone, and holy gost. JOHN FFERERE. xiij. meii, anno dni. MLVCIIIJ. in capella de Thorpe."

We summarize the service for habiting and blessing a hermit* from the pontifical of Bishop Lacy of Exeter, of the fourteenth century.† It begins with several psalms; then several short prayers for the incepting hermit, mentioning him by name.‡ Then follow two prayers for the benediction of his vestments, apparently for different parts of his habit; the first mentioning " hec indumenta humilitatem cordis et mundi contemptum signifi- cancia,"—these garments signifying humility of heart, and contempt of the world; the second blesses "hanc vestem pro conservande castitatis signo,"—this vestment the sign of chastity. The priest then delivers the vestments to the hermit kneeling before him, with these words, " Brother, behold we give to thee the eremitical habit (*habitum heremiticum*), with which we admonish thee to live henceforth chastely, soberly, and holily; in holy watchings, in fastings, in labours, in prayers, in works of mercy, that thou mayest have eternal life, and live for ever and ever." And he receives them saying, " Behold, I receive them in the name of the Lord; and promise myself so to do according to my power, the grace of God, and of the saints, helping me." Then he puts off his secular habit, the priest saying to him, " The Lord put off from thee the old man with his deeds; " and while he puts on his hermit's habit, the priest says, " The Lord put on thee the new man, which, after God, is created in righteousness and true holiness." Then follow a collect and certain psalms, and finally the priest sprinkles him with holy water, and blesses him.

Men of all ranks took upon them the hermit life, and we find the popular writers of the time sometimes distinguishing among them; one is a " hermit-priest,"§ another is a " gentle hermit," not in the sense of the

---

* " Officium induendi et benedicendi heremitam."

† We are indebted to Mr. M. H. Bloxam for a copy of it.

‡ " *Famulus tuus N.*" It is noticable that the masculine gender is used all through, without any such note as we find in the Service for Inclosing (which we shall have to notice hereafter), that this service shall serve for both sexes.

§ The hermit who interposed between Sir Lionel and Sir Bors, and who was killed by Sir Lionel for his interference (Malory's " Prince Arthur," III , lxxix.), is called a "gentle hermit of the dale," but meaning that he was a man of gentle birth.   The hermit in whose hermitage Sir Launcelot passed long time is described as a " gentle hermit, which sometime was a noble knight and a great lord of possessions, and for great goodness he hath taken him unto wilful poverty, and hath forsaken his possessions, and his name is Sir Baldwin of Britain, and he is a full noble surgeon, and a right good leech." This was the type of hermit who was venerated by the popular superstition of the day : a great and rich man who had taken to wilful poverty, or a man who lived wild in the woods—a St. Julian, or a St. Anthony. A poor man who turned hermit, and lived a prosaic, pious, useful life, showing travellers the way through a forest, or over a bog, or across a ferry, and humbly taking their alms in return, presented nothing dramatic and striking to the popular mind ; very likely, too, many men adopted the hermit life for the sake of the idleness and the alms,* and deserved the small repute they had.

It is *àpropos* of Sir Launcelot's hermit above-mentioned that the romancer complains " for in those days it was not with the guise of hermits as it now is in these days.   For there were no hermits in those days, but that they have been men of worship and prowess, and those hermits held great households, and refreshed people that were in distress."   We find the author of " Piers Ploughman " making the same complaint.   We have, as in other cases, a little modernised his language :—

> " But eremites that inhabit them by the highways,
> And in boroughs among brewers, and beg in churches,
> All that holy eremites hated and despised,
> (As riches, and reverences, and rich men's alms),
> These lollers,† latche drawers,‡ lewd eremites,

" hermit-priest."   Also, in the Episcopal Registry of Lichfield, we find the bishop, date 10th February, 1409, giving to Brother Richard Goldeston, late Canon of Wombrugge, now recluse at Prior's Lee, near Shiffenall, license to hear confessions.

* " Great loobies and long, that loath were to swink [work],
>   Clothed them in copes to be known from others,
>   And shaped them hermits their ease to have."

† Wanderers.   ‡ Breakers out of their cells.

Covet on the contrary.   Nor live holy as eremites,
That lived wild in woods, with bears and lions.
Some had livelihood from their lineage* and of no life else ;
And some lived by their learning, and the labour of their hands.
Some had foreigners for friends, that their food sent ;
And birds brought to some bread, whereby they lived.
All these holy eremites were of high kin,
Forsook land and lordship, and likings of the body.
But these eremites that edify by the highways
Whilome were workmen—webbers, and tailors,
And carter's knaves, and clerks without grace.
They held a hungry house,   And had much want,
Long labour, and light winnings.   And at last espied
That lazy fellows in friar's clothing had fat cheeks.
Forthwith left they their labour, these lewd knaves,
And clothed them in copes as they were clerks,
Or one of some order [of monks or friars], or else prophets [eremites]."

This curious extract from "Piers Ploughman" leads us to notice the localities in which hermitages were situated.   Sometimes, no doubt, they were in lonely and retired places among the hills, or hidden in the depths of the forests which then covered so large a portion of the land.   On the next page is a very interesting little picture of hermit life, from a MS. Book of Hours, executed for Richard II. (British Museum, Domitian, A. xvii., folio 4 v.)   The artist probably intended to represent the old hermits of the Egyptian desert, Piers Poughman's—

" Holy eremites,
That lived wild in woods
With bears and lions ;"

but, after the custom of mediæval art, he has introduced the scenery, costume, and architecture of his own time.   Erase the bears, which stand for the whole tribe of outlandish beasts, and we have a very pretty bit of English mountain scenery.   The stags are characteristic enough of the scenery of mediæval England.   The hermitage on the right seems to be of the ruder sort, made in part of wattled work.   On the left we have the more usual hermitage of stone, with its little chapel bell in a bell-cot on the gable. The venerable old hermit, coming out of the doorway, is a charming illus-

* Kindred.

tration of the typical hermit, with his venerable beard, and his form bowed by age, leaning with one hand on his cross-staff, and carrying his rosary in the other. The hermit in the illustration hereafter given from the "History of Launcelot," on page 114, leans on a similar staff; it would seem as if such a staff was a usual part of the hermit's equipment.* The hermit in Albert Dürer's "St. Christopher." already

Hermits and Hermitages.

mentioned, also leans on a staff, but of rather different shape. Here is a companion-picture, in pen and ink, from the "Morte d'Arthur : "—" Then he departed from the cross [a stone cross which parted two ways in waste land, under which he had been sleeping], on foot, into a wild forest. And so by prime he came unto an high mountain, and there he found an hermitage,

---

* In " Piers Ploughman " we read that—

" Hermits with hoked staves
Wenden to Walsingham ;"

These hooked staves may, however, have been pilgrim staves, not hermit staves. The pastoral staff on the official seal of Odo, Bishop of Bayeux, was of the same shape as the staff above represented. A staff of similar shape occurs on an early grave-stone at Welbeck Priory, engraved in the Rev. E. L. Cutts's " Manual of Sepulchral Slabs and Crosses," plate xxxv.

and an hermit therein, which was going to mass. And then Sir Launcelot kneeled down upon both his knees, and cried out, 'Lord, mercy!' for his wicked works that he had done. So when mass was done, Sir Launcelot called the hermit to him, and prayed him for charity to hear his confession. 'With a good will,' said the good man."

But many of the hermitages were erected along the great highways of the country, and especially at bridges and fords,* apparently with the express view of their being serviceable to travellers. One of the hermit-saints set up as a pattern for their imitation was St. Julian, who, with his wife, devoted his property and life to showing hospitality to travellers ; and the hermit who is always associated in the legends and pictures with St. Christopher, is represented as holding out his torch or lantern to light the giant ferryman, as he transports his passengers across the dangerous ford by which the hermitage was built. When hostelries, where the traveller could command entertainment for hire, were to be found only in the great towns, the religious houses were the chief resting-places of the traveller ; not only the conventual establishments, but the country clergy also were expected to be given to hospitality.† But both monasteries and country parsonages often lay at a distance of miles of miry and intricate by-road off the highway. We must picture this state of the country and of society to ourselves, before we can appreciate the intentions of those who founded these hospitable establishments ; we must try to imagine ourselves travellers, getting belated in a dreary part of the road, where it ran over a bleak wold, or dived through a dark forest, or approached an unknown ford, before we can appreciate the gratitude of those who suddenly caught

---

* Blomfield, in his "History of Norfolk," 1532, says, "It is to be observed that hermitages were erected, for the most part, near great bridges (see *Mag. Brit.*, On War-wickshire, p. 597, Dugdale, &c., and Badwell's 'Description of Tottenham') and high roads, as appears from this, and those at Brandon, Downham, Stow Bardolph, in Norfolk, and Erith, in the Isle of Ely, &c."

† In the settlement of the vicarage of Kelvedon, Essex, when the rectory was impro-priated to the abbot and convent of Westminster, in the fourteenth century, it was expressly ordered that the convent, besides providing the vicar a suitable house, should also provide a hall for receiving guests. See subsequent chapter on the Secular Clergy.

the light from the hermit's window, or heard the faint tinkle of his chapel bell ringing for vespers.

Such incidents occur frequently in the romances. Here is an example :— " Sir Launcelot rode all that day and all that night in a forest; and at the last, he was ware of an hermitage and a chapel that stood between two cliffs ; and then he heard a little bell ring to mass, and thither he rode, and alighted, and tied his horse to the gate, and heard mass." Again : " Sir Gawayne rode till he came to an hermitage, and there he found the good man saying his even-song of our Lady. And there Sir Gawayne asked harbour for charity, and the good man granted it him gladly."

We shall, perhaps, most outrage the popular idea of a hermit, when we assert that hermits sometimes lived in towns. The extract from " Piers Ploughman's Vision," already quoted, tells us of—

> " Eremites that inhabit them
> In boroughs among brewers."

The difficulty of distinguishing between hermits proper and recluses becomes very perplexing in this part of our subject. There is abundant proof, which we shall have occasion to give later, that recluses, both male and female, usually lived in towns and villages, and these recluses are sometimes called hermits, as well as by their more usual and peculiar name of anchorites and anchoresses. But we are inclined to the opinion, that not all the male solitaries who lived in towns were recluses. The author of " Piers Ploughman's Vision " speaks of the eremites who inhabited in boroughs as if they were of the same class as those who lived by the highways, and who ought to have lived in the wildernesses, like St. Anthony. The theory under which it was made possible for a solitary, an eremite, a man of the desert, to live in a town, was, that a churchyard formed a solitary place —a desert—within the town. The curious history which we are going to relate, seems to refer to hermits, not to recluses. The Mayor of Sudbury, under date January 28, 1433, petitioned the Bishop of Norwich, setting forth that the bishop had refused to admit " Richard Appleby, of Sudbury, conversant with John Levynton, of the same town, heremyte, to the order of Hermits, unless he was sure to be inhabited in a solitary place where virtues might be increased, and vice exiled;" and that therefore "we have granted hym, be the assent of all the sayd parish and cherch reves, to be inhabited with the sayd John Levynton in his solitary place and hermytage, whych y^t is made at the cost of the parysh, in the cherchyard of St. Gregory Cherche, to dwellen togedyr as (long as) yey liven, or whiche of them longest liveth;" and thereupon the mayor prays the bishop to admit Richard Appleby to the order.

This curious incident of two solitaries living together has a parallel in the romance of "King Arthur." When the bold Sir Bedivere had lost his lord King Arthur, he rode away, and, after some adventures, came to a chapel and an hermitage between two hills, "and he prayed the hermit that he might abide there still with him, to live with fasting and prayers. So Sir Bedivere abode there still with the hermit; and there Sir Bedivere put upon him poor clothes, and served the hermit full lowly in fasting and in prayers." And afterwards (as we have already related) Sir Launcelot "rode all that day and all that night in a forest. And at the last he was ware of an hermitage and a chapel that stood between two cliffs, and then he heard a little bell ring to mass; and thither he rode, and alighted, and tied his horse to the gate and heard mass." He had stumbled upon the hermitage in which Sir Bedivere was living. And when Sir Bedivere had made himself known, and had "told him his tale all whole," "Sir Launcelot's heart almost burst for sorrow, and Sir Launcelot threw abroad his armour, and said,—'Alas! who may trust this world?' And then he kneeled down on his knees, and prayed the hermit for to shrive him and assoil him. And then he besought the hermit that he might be his brother. And he put an habit upon Sir Launcelot, and there he served God day and night with prayers and fastings." And afterwards Sir Bors came in the same way. And within half a year there was come Sir Galahad, Sir Galiodin, Sir Bleoberis, Sir Villiers, Sir Clarus, and Sir Gahalatine. "So these seven noble knights abode there still: and when they saw that Sir Launcelot had taken him unto such perfection, they had no list to depart, but took such an habit as he had. Thus they endured in great penance six years, and then Sir Launcelot took the habit of priesthood, and twelve months he sung the mass; and there was none of these other

knights but that they read in books, and helped for to sing mass, and ring
bells, and did lowly all manner of service. And so their horses went
where they would, for they took no regard in worldly riches." And after a
little time Sir Launcelot died at the hermitage : "then was there weeping
and wringing of hands, and the greatest dole they made that ever made
man. And on the morrow the bishop-hermit sung his mass of requiem."
The accompanying wood-cut, from one of the small compartments at the
bottom of Cosimo Roselli's picture of St. Jerome, from which we have
already taken the figure of St. Damasus, may serve to illustrate this

Funeral Service of a Hermit.

incident. It represents a number of hermits mourning over one of their
brethren, while a priest in the robes proper to his office, stands at the
head of the bier and says prayers, and his deacon stands at the foot, holding a processional cross. The contrast between the robes of the priest
and those of the hermits is lost in the woodcut ; in the original the priest's
cope and amys are coloured red, while those of the hermits are tinted with
light brown.

If the reader has wondered how the one hermitage could accommodate
these seven additional habitants, the romancer does not forget to satisfy

his curiosity : a few pages farther we read—"So at the season of the night they went all to their beds, for they all lay in one chamber." It was not very unusual for hermitages to be built for more than one occupant ; but probably, in all such cases, each hermit had his own cell, adjoining their common chapel. This was the original arrangement of the hermits of the Thebais in their laura. The great difference between a hermitage with more than one hermit, and a small cell of one of the other religious orders, was that in such a cell one monk or friar would have been the prior, and the others subject to him ; but each hermit was independent of any authority on the part of the other ; he was subject only to the obligation of his rule, and the visitation of his bishop.

The life * of the famous hermit, Richard of Hampole, which has lately been published for the first time by the Early English Text Society, will enable us to realise in some detail the character and life of a mediæval hermit of the highest type. Saint Richard was born † in the village of Thornton, in Yorkshire. At a suitable age he was sent to school by the care of his parents, and afterwards was sent by Richard Neville, Archdeacon of Durham, to Oxford, where he gave himself specially to theological study. At the age of nineteen, considering the uncertainty of life and the awfulness of judgment, especially to those who waste life in pleasure or spend it in acquiring wealth, and fearing lest he should fall into such courses, he left Oxford and returned to his father's house. One day he asked of his sister two of her gowns (tunicas), one white, the other grey, and a cloak and hood of his father's. He cut up the two gowns, and fashioned out of them and of the hooded cloak an imitation of a hermit's habit, and next day he went off into a neighbouring wood bent upon living a hermit life. Soon after, on the vigil of the Assumption of the Blessed Virgin, he went to a certain church, and knelt down to pray in the place which the wife of a certain worthy knight, John de Dalton, was accustomed to occupy. When the lady came to church, her servants would have turned out the intruder, but she would not permit it. When vespers were over and he rose from his

---

* From the " Officium et Legenda de Vita Ricardi Rolle."
† When is not stated ; he died in 1349.

knees, the sons of Sir John, who were students at Oxford, recognised him as the son of William Rolle, whom they had known at Oxford. Next day Richard again went to the same church, and without any bidding put on a surplice and sang mattins and the office of the mass with the rest. And when the gospel was to be read at mass, he sought the blessing of the priest, and then entered the pulpit and preached a sermon to the people of such wonderful edification that many were touched with compunction even to tears, and all said they had never heard before a sermon of such power and efficacy. After mass Sir John Dalton invited him to dinner. When he entered into the manor he took his place in a ruined building, and would not enter the hall, according to the evangelical precept, "When thou art bidden to a wedding sit down in the lowest room, and when he that hath bidden thee shall see it he will say to thee, Friend, go up higher ;" which was fulfilled in him, for the knight made him sit at table with his own sons. But he kept such silence at dinner that he did not speak one word ; and when he had eaten sufficiently he rose before they took away the table and would have departed, but the knight told him this was contrary to custom, and made him sit down again. After dinner the knight had some private conversation with him, and being satisfied that he was not a madman, but really seemed to have the vocation to a hermit's life, he clothed him at his own cost in a hermit's habit, and retained him a long time in his own house, giving him a solitary chamber (*locum mansionis solitariæ*)* and providing him with all necessaries. Our hermit then gave himself up to ascetic discipline and a contemplative life. He wrote books; he counselled those who came to him. He did both at the same time ; for one afternoon the lady of the house

---

* Afterwards it is described as a cell at a distance from the family, where he was accustomed to sit solitary and to pass his time in contemplation. In doing this Sir John Dalton and his wife were, according to the sentiment of the time, following the example of the Shunammite and her husband, who made for Elisha a little chamber on the wall, and set for him there a bed, and a table, and a stool, and a candlestick (2 Kings iv. 10). The Knight of La Tour Landry illustrates this when in one of his tales (ch. xcv.) he describes the Shunammite's act in the language of mediæval custom : "This good woman had gret devocion unto this holy man, and required and praied hym for to come to her burghe and loged in her hous, and her husbonde and she made a chambre solitaire for this holy man, where as he might use his devocions and serve God."

came to him with many other persons and found him writing very rapidly, and begged him to stop writing and speak some words of edification to them ; and he began at once and continued to address them for two hours with admirable exhortations to cultivate virtue and to put away worldly vanities, and to increase the love of their hearts for God ; but at the same time he went on writing as fast as before. He used to be so absorbed in prayer that his friends took off his torn cloak, and when it had been mended put it on him again, without his knowing it. Soon we hear of his having temptations like those which assailed St. Anthony, the devil tempting him in the form of a beautiful woman. He was specially desirous to help recluses and those who required spiritual consolation, and who were vexed by evil spirits.

At length Lady Dalton died, and (whether as a result of this is not stated) the hermit left his cell and began to move from place to place. One time he came near the cell of Dame Margaret, the recluse of Anderby in Richmond-shire, and was told that she was dumb and suffering from some strange disease, and went to her. And he sat down at the window of the house of the recluse,* and when they had eaten, the recluse felt a desire to sleep ; and being oppressed with sleep her head fell towards the window at which St. Richard was reclined. And when she had slept a little, leaning some-what on Richard, suddenly she was seized with a convulsion, and awoke with her power of speech restored.

He wrote many works of ascetic and mystical divinity which were greatly esteemed. The Early English Text Society has published some specimens in the work from which these notices are gathered, which show that his reputation as a devotional writer was not undeserved. At length he settled at Hampole, where was a Cistercian nunnery. Here he died, and in the church of the nunnery he was buried. We are indebted for the Officium and Legenda from which we have gathered this outline of his life to the pious care of the nuns of Hampole, to whom the fame of Richard's sanctity was a source of great profit and honour. That he had a line of

---

* Either the little window through which she communicated with the outer world, or perhaps (as suggested further on) a window between her cell and a guest-chamber in which she received visitors.

successors in his anchorage is indicated by the fact hereafter stated (p. 128), that in 1415 A.D., Lord Scrope left by will a bequest to Elizabeth, late servant to the anchoret of Hampole.

There are indications that these hermitages were sometimes mere bothies of branches ; there is a representation of one, from which we here give a woodcut, in an illuminated MS. romance of Sir Launcelot, of early fourteenth-century date (British Museum, Add. 10,293, folio 118 v., date 1316) : we have already noticed another of wattled work.*   There are also

Sir Launcelot and a Hermit.

caves † here and there in the country which are said by tradition to have been hermitages : one is described in the *Archæological Journal,* vol. iv., p. 150. It is a small cave, not easy of access, in the side of a hill called Carcliff Tor, near Rowsley, a little miserable village not far from Haddon Hall. In a recess, on the right side as you enter the cave, is a crucifix about four feet high, sculptured in bold relief in the red grit rock out of

---

* A hermitage, partly of stone, partly of timber, may be seen in the beautiful MS. Egerton 1,147, f. 218 v.

† A very good representation of a cave hermitage may be found in the late MS. Egerton, 2,125, f. 206 v. Also in the Harl. MS. 1,527, at f. 14 v., is a hermit in a cave ; and in Royal 10 E IV. f. 130, here a man is bringing the hermit food and drink.

which the cave is hollowed ; and close to it, on the right, is a rude niche, perhaps to hold a lamp.

St. Robert's Chapel, at Knaresborough, Yorkshire, is a very excellent example of a hermitage.* It is hewn out of the rock, at the bottom of a cliff, in the corner of a sequestered dell. The exterior, a view of which is given below, presents us with a simply arched doorway at the bottom of

Exterior View of St. Robert's Chapel, Knaresborough.

the rough cliff, with an arched window on the left, and a little square opening between, which looks like the little square window of a recluse. Internally we find the cell sculptured into the fashion of a little chapel, with a groined ceiling, the groining shafts and ribs well enough designed, but rather rudely executed. There is a semi-octagonal apsidal recess at the east end, in which the altar stands ; a piscina and a credence and stone seat in the north wall; a row of sculptured heads in the south wall, and a grave-stone in the middle of the floor. This chapel appears to have been

---

* Eugene Aram's famous murder was perpetrated within it. See Sir E. L. Bulwer's description of the scene in his "Eugene Aram."

also the hermit's living room.   The view of the exterior, and of the interior and ground-plan, are from Carter's "Ancient Architecture," pl. lxvii. Another hermitage, whose chapel is very similar to this, is at Warkworth. It is half-way up the cliff, on one side of a deep, romantic valley, through which runs the river Coquet, overhung with woods.   The chapel is hewn out of the rock, 18 feet long by 7½ wide, with a little entrance-porch on the south, also hewn in the rock; and, on the farther side, a long, narrow

Interior View of St. Robert's Chapel.

apartment, with a small altar at the east end, and a window looking upon the chapel altar.   This long apartment was probably the hermit's living room; but when the Earls of Northumberland endowed the hermitage for a chantry priest, the priest seems to have lived in a small house, with a garden attached, at the foot of the cliff.   The chapel is groined, and has Gothic windows, very like that of Knaresborough.   A minute description of this hermitage, and of the legend connected with it, is given in a poem called "The History of Warkworth" (4to, 1775), and in a letter in Grose's "Antiquities," vol. iii., is a ground-plan of the chapel and its appurtenances.

A view of the exterior, showing its picturesque situation, will be found in Herne's "Antiquities of Great Britain," pl. 9.

There is a little cell, or oratory, called the hermitage, cut out of the face of a rock near Dale Abbey, Derbyshire. On the south side are the door and three windows; at the east end, an altar standing upon a raised platform, both cut out of the rock; there are little niches in the walls, and a stone seat all round.*

There is another hermitage of three cells at Wetheral, near Carlisle, called Wetheral Safeguard, or St. Constantine's Cells—Wetheral Priory was dedicated to St. Constantine, and this hermitage seems to have belonged to the priory. It is not far from Wetheral Priory, in the face of a rock standing 100 feet perpendicularly out of the river Eden, which washes its base; the hill rising several hundred feet higher still above this rocky escarpment. The hermitage is at a height of 40 feet from the river, and can only be approached from above by a narrow and difficult path down the face of the precipice. It consists of three square cells, close together, about 10 feet square and 8 feet high; each with

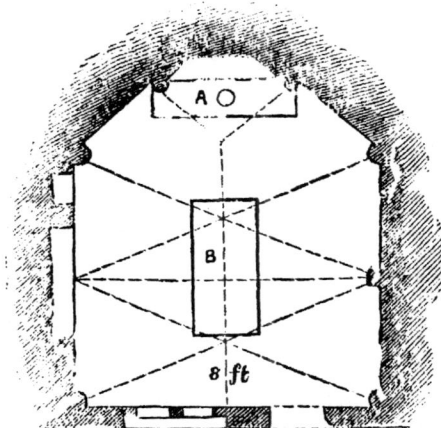

Ground-Plan of St. Robert's Chapel.

a short passage leading to it, which increases its total length to about 20 feet. These passages communicate with a little platform of rock in front of the cells. At a lower level than this platform, by about 7 feet, there is a narrow gallery built up of masonry; the door to the hermitage is at one end of it, so that access to the cells can only be obtained by means of a ladder from this gallery to the platform of rock 7 feet above it. In the front of the gallery are three windows, opposite to the three cells, to give them light, and one chimney. An engraving will be found in Hutchinson's "History of Cumberland," vol. i. p. 160, which

---

* See view in Stukeley's "Itin. Curios.," pl. 14.

I

shows the picturesque scene—the rocky hill-side, with the river washing round its base, and the three windows of the hermitage, half-way up, peeping through the foliage ; there is also a careful plan of the cells in the letterpress.

A chapel, and a range of rooms—which communicate with one another, and form a tolerably commodious house of two floors, are excavated out of a rocky hill-side, called Blackstone Rock, which forms the bank of the Severn, near Bewdley, Worcestershire. A view of the exterior of the rock, and a plan and section of the chambers, are given both in Stukeley's

"Itinerarium Curiosum," pls. 13 and 14, and in Nash's "History of Worcestershire," vol. ii. p. 48.

At Lenton, near Nottingham, there is a chapel and a range of cells excavated out of the face of a semicircular sweep of rock, which crops out on the bank of the river Leen. The river winds round the other semicircle, leaving a space of greensward between the rock and the river, upon which the cells open. Now, the whole place is enclosed, and used as a public garden and bowling-green, its original features being, however, preserved with a praiseworthy appreciation of their interest. In former days this hermitage was just within the verge of the park of the royal castle of Nottingham ; it was doubtless screened by the trees of the park ; and its inmates might pace to and fro on their secluded grass-plot, fenced in by the rock and the river from every intruding foot, and yet in full view of the walls and towers of the castle, with the royal banner waving from its keep, and catch a glimpse of the populous borough, and see the parties of knights and ladies prance over the level meadows which stretched out to the neighbouring Trent like a green carpet, embroidered in spring and autumn by the purple crocus, which grows wild there in myriads. Stukeley, in his " Itinerarium Curiosum," pl. 39, gives a view and ground-plan of these curious cells. Carter also figures them in his " Ancient Architecture," pl. 12, and gives details of a Norman shaft and arch in the chapel.

But nearly all the hermitages which we read of in the romances, or see depicted in the illuminations and paintings, or find noticed in ancient historical documents, are substantial buildings of stone or timber. Here is one from folio 56 of the " History of Launcelot " (Add. 10,293) : the hermit stands at the door of his house, giving his parting benediction to Sir Launcelot, who, with his attendant physician, is taking his leave after a night's sojourn at the hermitage. In the paintings of the Campo Santo, at Pisa (engraved in Mrs. Jameson's " Sacred and Legendary Art "), which represent the hermits of the Egyptian desert, some of the hermitages are caves, some are little houses of stone. In Caxton's " Vitas Patrum " the hermitages are little houses ; one has a stepped gable ; another is like a gateway, with a room over it.* They were founded and built, and often endowed, by the same men who founded chantries, and built churches, and endowed monasteries ; and from the same motives of piety, charity, or superstition. And the founders seem often to have retained the patronage of the hermitages, as of valuable benefices, in their own hands.† A hermit-

---

* Suggesting the room so often found over a church porch.

† In the year 1490, a dispute having arisen between the abbot and convent of Easby and the Grey Friars of Richmond, on the one part, and the burgesses of Richmond, on the other part, respecting the disposition of the goods of Margaret Richmond, late anchoress of the same town, it was at length settled that the goods should remain with the warden and brethren of the friars, after that her debts and the repair of the anchorage were defrayed, " because the said anchoress took her habit of the said friars," and that the abbot and convent should have the disposition of the then anchoress, Alison

age was, in fact, a miniature monastery, inhabited by one religious, who was abbot, and prior, and convent, all in one : sometimes also by a chaplain,* where the hermit was not a priest, and by several lay brethren, *i.e.* servants. It had a chapel of its own, in which divine service was performed daily. It had also the apartments necessary for the accommodation of the hermit, and his chaplain—when one lived in the hermitage—and his servants, and the necessary accommodation for travellers besides ; and it had often, perhaps generally, its court-yard and garden.

The chapel of the hermitage seems not to have been appropriated solely to the performance of divine offices, but to have been made useful for other more secular purposes also. Indeed, the churches and chapels in the Middle Ages seem often to have been used for great occasions of a semi-religious character, when a large apartment was requisite, *e.g.* for holding councils, for judicial proceedings, and the like. Godric of Finchale, a hermit who lived about the time of Henry II.,† had two chapels adjoining his cell ; one he called by the name of St. John Baptist, the other after the Blessed Virgin. He had a kind of common room, " communis domus," in which he cooked his food and saw visitors; but he lived chiefly, day and night, in the chapel of St. John, removing his bed to the chapel of St. Mary at times of more solemn devotion.

In an illumination on folio 153 of the " History of Launcelot," already quoted (British Mus., Add. 10,293), is a picture of King Arthur taking

---

Comeston, after her decease; and so to continue for evermore between the said abbot and warden, as it happens that the anchoress took her habit of religion. And that the burgesses shall have the nomination and free election of the said anchoress for evermore from time to time when it happens to be void, as they have had without time of mind. (Test. Ebor. ii. 115.)

* In June 5, 1356, Edward III. granted to brother Regnier, hermit of the Chapel of St. Mary Magdalen, without Salop, a certain plot of waste called Shelcrosse, contiguous to the chapel, containing one acre, to hold the same to him and his successors, hermits there, for their habitation, and to find a chaplain to pray in the chapel for the king's soul, &c. (Owen and Blakeway's " History of Shrewsbury," vol. ii. p. 165). " Perhaps," say our authors, " this was the eremitical habitation in the wood of Suttona (Sutton being a village just without Salop), which is recorded elsewhere to have been given by Richard, the Dapifer of Chester, to the monks of Salop."

† " Vita S. Godrici," published by the Surtees Society.

counsel with a hermit in his hermitage. The building in which they are seated has a nave and aisles, a rose-window in its gable, and a bell-turret, and seems intended to represent the chapel of the hermitage. Again, at folio 107 of the same MS. is a picture of a hermit talking to a man, with the title,—"Ensi y come une hermites prole en une chapele de son hermitage,"—" How a hermit conversed in the chapel of his hermitage." It may, perhaps, have been in the chapel that the hermit received those who sought his counsel on spiritual or on secular affairs.

In addition to the references which have already been given to illus‑ trations of the subject in the illuminations of MSS., we call the special attention of the student to a series of pictures illustrating a mediæval story of which a hermit is the hero, in the late thirteenth century MS. Royal 10 E IV.; it begins at folio 113 v., and runs on for many pages, and is full of interesting passages.

We also add a few lines from Lydgate's unpublished "Life of St. Edmund," as a typical picture of a hermit, drawn in the second quarter of the fifteenth century :—

"— holy Ffremund though he were yonge of age,
And ther he bilte a litel hermitage
Be side a ryver with al his besy peyne,
He and his fellawis that were in nombre tweyne.

"A litel chapel he dide ther edifie,
Day be day to make in his praiere,
In the reverence only off Marie
And in the worshipe of her Sone deere,
And the space fully off sevene yeere
Hooly Ffremund, lik as it is founde,
Leved be frut and rootes off the grounde.

"Off frutes wilde, his story doth us telle,
Was his repast penance for t' endure,
To stanch his thurst drank water off the welle
And eet acorns to sustene his nature,
Kernelles off notis [nuts] when he myhte hem recure.
To God alway doying reverence,
What ever he sent took it in patience."

And in concluding this chapter let us call to mind Spenser's description of a typical hermit and hermitage, while the originals still lingered in the living memory of the people :—

"At length they chaunst to meet upon the way
An aged sire, in long blacke weedes yclad,
His feet all bare, his head all hoarie gray,
And by his belt his booke he hanging had ;
Sober he seemde, and very sagely sad,
And to the ground his eyes were lowly bent,
Simple in shew, and voide of malice bad ;
And all the way he prayed as he went,
And often knockt his brest as one that did repent.

"He faire the knight saluted, louting low,
Who faire him quited, as that courteous was ;
And after asked him if he did know
Of strange adventures which abroad did pas.
'Ah ! my dear sonne,' quoth he, 'how should, alas !
Silly* old man, that lives in hidden cell,
Bidding his beades all day for his trespas,
Tidings of war and worldly trouble tell ?
With holy father sits not with such things to mell.'†
   *   *   *   *   *   *
Quoth then that aged man, 'The way to win
Is wisely to advise. Now day is spent,
Therefore with me ye may take up your in
For this same night.' The knight was well content;
So with that godly father to his home he went.

"A little lowly hermitage it was,
Down in a dale, hard by a forest's side,
Far from resort of people that did pass
In traveill to and froe ; a little wyde
There was an holy chappell edifyde,
Wherein the hermite dewly wont to say
His holy things, each morne and eventyde ;
Hereby a chrystall streame did gently play,
Which from a sacred fountaine welled forth alway.

"Arrived there, the little house they fill ;
Ne look for entertainment where none was ;
Rest is their feast, and all things at their will:
The noblest mind the best contentment has.
With fair discourse the evening so they pas ;
For that old man of pleasing words had store,
And well could file his tongue as smooth as glas;

* Simple.   † Meddle.

He told of saintes and popes, and evermore
He strowd an Ave-Mary after and before."*
Faery Queen, i. 1, 29, 33, 34, 35.

* Since the above was written, the writer has had an opportunity of visiting a hermitage very like those at Warkworth, Wetheral, Bewdley, and Lenton, still in use and habitation. It is in the parish of Limay, near Mantes, a pretty little town on the railway between Rouen and Paris. Nearly at the top of a vine-clad hill, on the north of the valley of the Seine, in which Mantes is situated, a low face of rock crops out. In this rock have been excavated a chapel, a sacristy, and a living-room for the hermit; and the present hermit has had a long refectory added to his establishment, in which to give his annual dinner to the people who come here, one day in the year, in considerable numbers, on pilgrimage. The chapel differs from those which we have described in the text in being larger and ruder; it is so wide that its rocky roof is supported by two rows of rude pillars, left standing for that purpose by the excavators. There is an altar at the east end. At the west end is a representation of the Entombment; the figure of our Lord, lying as if it had become rigid in the midst of the writhing of his agony, is not without a rude force of expression. One of the group of figures standing about the tomb has a late thirteenth-century head of a saint placed upon the body of a Roman soldier of the Renaissance period. There is a grave-stone with an incised cross and inscription beside the tomb; and in the niche on the north side is a recumbent monumental effigy of stone, with the head and hands in white glazed pottery. But whether these things were originally placed in the hermitage, or whether they are waifs and strays from neighbouring churches, brought here as to an ecclesiastical peep-show, it is hard to determine; the profusion of other incongruous odds and ends of ecclesiastical relics and fineries, with which the whole place is furnished, inclines one to the latter conjecture. There is a bell-turret built on the rock over the chapel, and a chimney peeps through the hill-side, over the sacristy fireplace. The platform in front of the hermitage is walled in, and there is a little garden on the hill above. The curé of Limay performs service here on certain days in the year. The hermit will disappoint those who desire to see a modern example of

" An aged sire, in long black weedes yclad,
His feet all bare, his beard all hoarie gray."

He is an aged sire, seventy-four years old; but for the rest, he is simply a little, withered, old French peasant, in a blue blouse and wooden sabots. He passes his days here in solitude, unless when a rare party of visitors ring at his little bell, and, after due inspection through his *grille*, are admitted to peep about his chapel and his grotto, and to share his fine view of the valley shut in by vine-clad hills, and the Seine winding through the flat meadows, and the clean, pretty town of Mantes *le jolie* in the middle, with its long bridge and its cathedral-like church. Whether he spends his time

" Bidding his beades all day for his trespas,"

we did not inquire; but he finds the hours lonely. The good curé of Limay wishes him to sleep in his hermitage, but, like the hermit-priest of Warkworth, he prefers sleeping in the village at the foot of the hill.

CHAPTER II.

ANCHORESSES, OR FEMALE RECLUSES.

AND now we proceed to speak more particularly of the recluses. The old legend tells us that John the Hermit, the contemporary of St. Anthony, would hold communication with no man except through the window of his cell.* But the recluses of more modern days were not content to quote John the Egyptian as their founder. As the Carmelite friars claimed Elijah, so the recluses, at least the female recluses, looked up to Judith as the foundress of their mode of life, and patroness of their order.

Mabillon tells us that the first who made any formal rule for recluses was one Grimlac, who lived about 900 A.D. The principal regulations of his rule are, that the candidate for reclusion, if a monk, should signify his intention a year beforehand, and during the interval should continue to live among his brethren. If not already a monk, the period of probation was doubled. The leave of the bishop of the diocese was to be first obtained, and if the candidate were a monk, the leave of his abbot and convent also. When he had entered his cell, the bishop was to put his seal upon the door, which was never again to be opened,† unless for the

---

* One of the little hermitages represented in the Campo Santo series of paintings of the old Egyptian hermit-saints (engraved in Mrs. Jameson's "Legends of the Monastic Orders") has a little grated window, through which the hermit within (probably this John) is talking with another outside.

† That recluses did, however, sometimes quit their cells on a great emergency, we learn from the Legenda of Richard of Hampole already quoted, where we are told that at his death Dame Margaret Kyrkley, the recluse of Anderby, on hearing of the saint's death, hastened to Hampole to be present at his funeral.

help of the recluse in time of sickness or on the approach of death. Successive councils published canons to regulate this kind of life. That of Millo, in 692, repeats in substance the rule of Grimlac. That of Frankfort, in 787, refers to the recluses. The synod of Richard de la Wich, Bishop of Chichester, A.D. 1246, makes some canons concerning them : " Also we ordain to recluses that they shall not receive or keep any person in their houses concerning whom any sinister suspicion might arise. Also that they have narrow and proper windows ; and we permit them to have secret communication with those persons only whose gravity and honesty do not admit of suspicion." *

Towards the end of the twelfth century a rule for anchorites was written by Bishop Richard Poore† of Chichester, and afterwards of Salisbury, who died A.D. 1237, which throws abundant light upon their mode of life ; for it is not merely a brief code of the regulations obligatory upon them, but it is a book of paternal counsels, which enters at great length, and in minute detail, into the circumstances of the recluse life, and will be of great use to us in the subsequent part of this chapter.

There were doubtless different degrees of austerity among the recluses ; but, on the whole, we must banish from our minds the popular ‡ idea that they inhabited a living grave, and lived a life of the extremest mortification. Doubtless there were instances in which religious enthusiasm led the

---

* Wilkins's " Concilia," i. 693.

† Several MSS. of this rule are known under different names. Fosbroke quotes one as the rule of Simon de Gandavo (or Simon of Ghent), in Cott. MS. Nero A xiv.; another in Bennet College, Cambridge ; and another under the name of Alfred Reevesley. See Fosbroke's " British Monachism," pp. 374-5. The various copies, indeed, seem to differ considerably, but to be all derived from the work ascribed to Bishop Poore. All these books are addressed to female recluses, which is a confirmation of the opinion which we have before expressed, that the majority of the recluses were women.

‡ Thus the player-queen in *Hamlet*, iii. 2 :—

> " Nor earth to me give food, nor heaven light !
> Sport and repose lock from me, day, and night !
> To desperation turn my trust and hope !
> An anchor's cheer in prison be my scope !
> Each opposite, that blanks the face of joy,
> Meet what I would have well, and it destroy," &c.

recluse into frightful and inhuman self-torture, like that of Thaysis, in the
" Golden Legend :" " She went to the place whiche th' abbot had assygned
to her, and there was a monasterye of vyrgyns ; and there he closed her
in a celle, and sealed the door with led. And the celle was lytyll and
strayte, and but one lytell wyndowe open, by whyche was mynistred to her
poor lyvinge ; for the abbot commanded that they shold gyve to her a
lytell brede and water."*   Thaysis submitted to it at the command of
Abbot Pafnucius, as penance for a sinful life, in the early days of Egyptian
austerity ; and now and then throughout the subsequent ages the self-
hatred of an earnest, impassioned nature, suddenly roused to a feeling of
exceeding sinfulness ; the remorse of a wild, strong spirit, conscious of great
crimes ; or the enthusiasm of a weak mind and morbid conscience, might
urge men and women to such self-revenges, to such penances, as these.
Bishop Poore gives us episodically a pathetic example, which our readers
will thank us for repeating here.   " Nothing is ever so hard that love doth
not make tender, and soft, and sweet. Love maketh all things easy.
What do men and women endure for false love, and would endure more !
And what is more to be wondered at is, that love which is faithful and
true, and sweeter than any other love, doth not overmaster us as doth
sinful love ! Yet I know a man who weareth at the same time both a
heavy cuirass† and haircloth, bound with iron round the middle too, and
his arms with broad and thick bands, so that to bear the sweat of it is
severe suffering.   He fasteth, he watcheth, he laboureth, and, Christ
knoweth, he complaineth, and saith that it doth not oppress him ; and
often asks me to teach him something wherewith he might give his body
pain. God knoweth that he, the most sorrowful of men, weepeth to me,
and saith that God hath quite forgotten him, because He sendeth him no
great sickness ; whatever is bitter seems sweet to him for our Lord's sake.
God knoweth love doth this, because, as he often saith to me, he could
never love God the less for any evil thing that He might do to him, even

---

* A cell in the north-west angle of Edington Abbey Church, Wilts, seems to be of
this kind.

† The wearing a cuirass, or hauberk of chain mail, next the skin became a noted form
of self-torture ; those who undertook it were called *Loricati.*

were He to cast him into hell with those that perish. And if any believe any such thing of him, he is more confounded than a thief taken with his theft. I know also a woman of like mind that suffereth little less. And what remaineth but to thank God for the strength that He giveth them ; and let us humbly acknowledge our own weakness, and love their merit, and thus it becomes our own. For as St. Gregory says, love is of so great power that it maketh the merit of others our own, without labour." But though powerful motives and great force of character might enable an individual here and there to persevere with such austerities, when the severities of the recluse life had to be reduced to rule and system, and when a succession of occupants had to be found for the vacant anchor-holds, ordinary human nature revolted from these unnatural austerities, and the common sense of mankind easily granted a tacit dispensation from them ; and the recluse life was speedily toned down in practice to a life which a religiously-minded person, especially one who had been wounded and worsted in the battle of life, might gladly embrace and easily endure.

Usually, even where the cell consisted of a single room, it was large enough for the comfortable abode of a single inmate, and it was not destitute of such furnishing as comfort required. But it was not unusual for the cell to be in fact a house of several apartments, with a garden attached ; and it would seem that the technical " cell " within which the recluse was immured, included house and garden, and everything within the boundary wall.* It is true that many of the recluses lived entirely, and perhaps all partly, upon the alms of pious and charitable people. An alms-box was hung up to receive contributions, as appears from " Piers Ploughman,"—

" In ancres there a box hangeth."

And in the extracts hereafter given from the "Ancren Riewle," we shall find several allusions to the giving of alms to recluses as a usual custom. But it was the bishop's duty, before giving license for the building of a reclusorium, to satisfy himself that there would be, either from alms or from an endowment, a sufficient maintenance for the recluse. Practically, they

* The cell of a Carthusian monk, as we have stated, consisted of a little house of three apartments and a little garden within an inclosure wall.

do not seem often to have been in want; they were restricted as to the times when they might eat flesh-meat, but otherwise their abstemiousness depended upon their own religious feeling on the subject; and the only check upon excess was in their own moderation. They occupied themselves, besides their frequent devotions, in reading, writing, illuminating, and needlework; and though the recluses attached to some monasteries seem to have been under an obligation of silence, yet in the usual case the recluse held a perpetual levee at the open window, and gossiping and scandal

Sir Percival at the Reclusorium.

appear to have been among her besetting sins. It will be our business to verify and further to illustrate this general sketch of the recluse life.

And, first, let us speak more in detail of their habitations. The reclusorium, or anchorhold, seems sometimes to have been, like the hermitage, a house of timber or stone, or a grotto in a solitary place. In Sir T. Mallory's " Prince Arthur " we are introduced to one of these, which afforded all the appliances for lodging and entertaining even male guests. We read :—" Sir Percival returned again unto the recluse, where he deemed to have tidings of that knight which Sir Launcelot followed. And so he kneeled at her window, and anon the recluse opened it, and asked Sir Percival what he would. ' Madam,' said he, ' I am a knight of King

Arthur's court, and my name is Sir Percival de Galis.' So when the recluse heard his name, she made passing great joy of him, for greatly she loved him before all other knights of the world ; and so of right she ought to do, for she was his aunt. And then she commanded that the gates should be opened to him, and then Sir Percival had all the cheer that she might make him, and all that was in her power was at his commandment." But it does not seem that she entertained him in person ; for the story continues that " on the morrow Sir Percival went unto the recluse," *i.e.*, to her little audience-window, to propound his question, " if she knew that knight with the white shield." Opposite is a woodcut of a picture in the MS. " History of Sir Launcelot " (Royal 14, E. III. folio 101 v.), entitled, " Ensi q Percheva retourna à la rencluse qui estait en son hermitage." *

In the case of these large remote anchorholds, the recluse must have had a chaplain to come and say mass for her every day in the chapel of her hermitage.† But in the vast majority of cases, anchorholds were attached to a church either of a religious house, or of a town, or of a village ; and in these situations they appear to have been much more numerous than is at all suspected by those who have not inquired into this little-known portion of our mediæval antiquities. Very many of our village churches had a recluse living within or beside them, and it will, perhaps, especially surprise the majority of our readers to learn that these recluses were specially numerous in the mediæval towns.‡ The proofs of this fact are abundant ; here are some. Henry, Lord Scrope, of Masham, by will, dated 23rd June, 1415, bequeathed to every anchoret§ and recluse dwelling in London or its suburbs 6s. 8d. ; also to every anchoret and recluse dwelling in York and its suburbs 6s. 8d. From other sources we learn more about

---

* This very same picture is given also in another MS. of about the same date, marked Add. 10,294, at folio 14.

† As was probably the case at Warkworth, the hermit living in the hermitage, while the chantry priest lived in the house at the foot of the hill.

‡ " Eremites that inhabiten
By the highways,
And in boroughs among brewers."
Piers Ploughman's Vision.

§ Probably " anchoret " means male, and "recluse " female recluse.

these York anchorets and recluses. The will of Adam Wigan, rector of St. Saviour, York (April 20, 1433, A.D.)*, leaves 3*s.* 4*d.* to Dan John, who dwelt in the Chapel of St. Martin, within the parish of St. Saviour. The female recluses of York were three in number in the year 1433, as we learn from the will of Margaret, relict of Nicholas Blackburne:† "Lego tribus reclusis Ebor.," ij*s.* Where their cells were situated we learn from the will of Richard Rupell (A.D. 1435 ‡), who bequeaths to the recluse in the cemetery of the Church of St. Margaret, York, five marks; and to the recluse in the cemetery of St. Helen, in Fishergate, five marks; and to the recluse in the cemetery of All Saints, in North Street, York, five marks. They are also all three mentioned in the will of Adam Wigan, who leaves to the anchorite enclosed in Fishergate 2*s.*; to her enclosed near the church of St. Margaret 2*s.*; to her enclosed in North Street, near the Church of All Saints, 2*s.* The will of Lady Margaret Stapelton, 1465 A.D.,§ mentions anchorites in Watergate and Fishergate, in the suburbs of York, and in another place the anchorite of the nunnery of St. Clement, York. At Lincoln, also, we are able to trace a similar succession of anchoresses. In 1383 A.D., William de Belay, of Lincoln, left to an anchoress named Isabella, who dwelt in the Church of the Holy Trinity, in Wigford, within the city of Lincoln, 13*s.* 4*d.* In 1391, John de Sutton left her 20*s.*; in 1374, John de Ramsay left her 12*d.* Besides these she had numerous other legacies from citizens. In 1453, an anchoress named Matilda supplied the place of Isabella, who we may suppose had long since gone to her reward. In that year John Tilney—one of the Tilneys of Boston—left "Domine Matilde incluse infra ecclesiam sanctæ Trinitatis ad gressus in civitate Lincoln, vj*s.* viij*d.*" In 1502, Master John Watson, a chaplain in Master Robert Flemyng's chantry, left xij*d.* to the "ankers" at the Greese foot. This Church of the Holy Trinity "ad gressus" seems to have been for a long period the abode of a female recluse.‖ The will of Roger Eston, rector of Richmond, Yorkshire, A.D. 1446, also mentions the recluses in the city of York and its suburbs. The

---

* Test. Vetust., ii. 25.   † Ibid. ii. 47.   ‡ Ibid. ii. 56.   § Ibid. ii. 271.
‖ Note p. 87 to "Instructions for Parish Priests," Early English Text Society.

will of Adam Wilson also mentions Lady Agnes, enclosed at (*apud*) the parish church of Thorganby, and anchorites (female) at Beston and Pontefract. Sir Hugh Willoughby, of Wollaton, in 1463 bequeathed 6*s.* 5*d.* to the anchoress of Nottingham.* The will of Lady Joan Wombewell, A.D. 1454,† also mentions the anchoress of Beyston. The will of John Brompton, of Beverley, A.D. 1444,‡ bequeaths 3*s.* 4*d.* to the recluse by the Church of St. Giles, and 1*s.* 6*d.* to anchorite at the friary of St. Nicholas of Beverley. Roger Eston also leaves a bequest to the anchorite of his parish of Richmond, respecting whom the editor gives a note whose substance is given elsewhere. In a will of the fifteenth century § we have a bequest " to the ancher in the wall beside Bishopsgate, London."‖ In the will of St. Richard, Bishop of Chichester,¶ we have bequests to Friar Humphrey, the recluse of Pageham, to the recluse of Hogton, to the recluse of Stopeham, to the recluse of Herringham; and in the will of Walter de Suffield, Bishop of Norwich, bequests to " anchers " and recluses in his diocese, and especially to his niece Ela, *in reclusorio* at Massingham.**

Among the other notices which we have of solitaries living in towns, Lydgate mentions one in the town of Wakefield. Morant says there was one in Holy Trinity churchyard, Colchester. The episcopal registers of Lichfield show that there was an anchorage for several female recluses in the churchyard of St. George's Chapel, Shrewsbury. The will of Henry, Lord Scrope, already quoted, leaves 100*s.* and the pair of beads which the testator was accustomed to use to the anchorite of Westminster: it was his predecessor, doubtless, who is mentioned in the time of Richard II.: when the young king was going to meet Wat Tyler in Smithfield, he went to Westminster Abbey, " then to the church, and so to the high altar, where he devoutly prayed and offered; after which he spake with the

---

* Test. Vetust., ii. 131. † Ibid. 178. ‡ Ibid. ii. 98. § Ibid. 356.

‖ Other bequests to recluses occur in the will of Henry II., to the recluses (*incluses*) of Jerusalem, England, and Normandy.

¶ Sussex Archæol. Coll., i. p. 174.

** Blomfield's " Norfolk," ii. pp. 347-8. See also the bequests to the Norwich recluses, *infra.*

anchore, to whom he confessed himself."* Lord Scrope's will goes on **to** bequeath 40*s.* to Robert, the recluse of Beverley; 13*s.* 4*d.* each to the anchorets of Stafford, of Kurkebeck, of Wath, of Peasholme, near York, of Kirby, Thorganby, near Colingworth, of Leek, near Upsale, of Gainsburgh, of Kneesall, near South Well, of Dartford, of Stamford, living in the parish church there; to Thomas, the chaplain dwelling continually in the church of St. Nicholas, Gloucester; to Elizabeth, late servant to the anchoret of Hamphole; and to the recluse in the house of the Dominicans at New-castle: and also 6*s.* 8*d.* to every other anchorite and anchoritess that could be easily found within three months of his decease.

We have already had occasion to mention that there were several female recluses, in addition to the male solitaries, in the churchyards of the then great city of Norwich. The particulars which that laborious antiquary, Blomfield, has collected together respecting several of them will throw a little additional light upon our subject, and fill up still further the out-lines of the picture which we are engaged in painting.

There was a hermitage in the churchyard of St. Julian, Norwich, which was inhabited by a succession of anchoresses, some of whose names Blom-field records:—Dame Agnes, in 1472; Dame Elizabeth Scot, in 1481; Lady Elizabeth, in 1510; Dame Agnes Edrigge, in 1524. The Lady Julian, who was the anchoress in 1393, is said to have had two servants to attend her in her old age. "She was esteemed of great holiness. Mr. Francis Peck had a vellum MS. containing an account of her visions." Blomfield says that the foundations of the anchorage might still be seen in his time, on the east side of St. Julian's churchyard. There was also an anchorage in St. Ethelred's churchyard, which was rebuilt in 1305, and an anchor continually dwelt there till the Reformation, when it was pulled down, and the grange, or tithe-barn, at Brakendale was built with its timber; so that it must have been a timber house of some magnitude. Also in St. Edward's churchyard, joining to the church on the north side, was a cell, whose ruins were still visible in Blomfield's time, and most per-sons who died in Norwich left small sums towards its maintenance. In

* Stow's Chronicle, p. 559.

1428 Lady Joan was anchoress here, to whom Walter Ledman left 20*s.*, and 40*d.* to each of her servants. In 1458, Dame Anneys Kite was the recluse here; in 1516, Margaret Norman, widow, was buried here, and gave a legacy to the lady anchoress by the church. St. John the Evangelist's Church, in Southgate, was, about A.D. 1300, annexed to the parish of St. Peter per Montergate, and the Grey Friars bought the site; they pulled down the whole building, except a small part left for an anchorage, in which they placed an anchor, to whom they assigned part of the churchyard for his garden. Also there used anciently to be a recluse dwelling in a little cell joining to the north side of the tower of St. John the Baptist's Church, Timber Hill, but it was down before the Dissolution. Also there was an anchor, or hermit, who had an anchorage in or adjoining to All Saints' Church. Also in Henry III.'s time a recluse dwelt in the churchyard of St. John the Baptist, and the Holy Sepulchre, in Ber Street. In the monastery of the Carmelites, or White Friars, at Norwich, there were two anchorages—one for a man, who was admitted brother of the house, and another for a woman, who was admitted sister thereof. The latter was under the chapel of the Holy Cross, which was still standing in Blomfield's time, though converted into dwelling-houses. The former stood by St. Martin's Bridge, on the east side of the street, and had a small garden to it, which ran down to the river. In 1442, December 2nd, the Lady Emma, recluse, or anchoress, and religious sister of the Carmelite order, was buried in their church. In 1443, Thomas Scroope was anchorite in this house. In 1465, Brother John Castleacre, a priest, was anchorite. In 1494 there were legacies given to the anchor of the White Friars. This Thomas Scroope was originally a Benedictine monk; in 1430 he became anchorite here (being received a brother of the Carmelite order), and led an anchorite's life for many years, seldom going out of his cell but when he preached; about 1446 Pope Eugenius made him Bishop of Down, which see he afterwards resigned, and came again to his convent, and became suffragan to the Bishop of Norwich. He died, and was buried at Lowestoft, being near a hundred years old.

The document which we are about to quote from Whittaker's " History of Whalley " (pp. 72 and 77), illustrates many points in the history of these anchorholds.   The anchorage therein mentioned was built in a parish churchyard, it depended upon a monastery, and was endowed with an allowance in money and kind from the monastery ; it was founded for two recluses ; they had a chaplain and servants ; and the patronage was retained by the founder.   The document will also give us some very curious and minute details of the domestic economy of the recluse life ; and, lastly, it will give us an historical proof that the assertions of the contemporary satirists, of the laxity* with which the vows were sometimes kept, were not without foundation.

" In 1349, Henry, Duke of Lancaster, granted in trust to the abbot and convent of Whalley rather large endowments to support two recluses (women) in a certain place within the churchyard of the parish church of Whalley, and two women servants to attend them, there to pray for the soul of the duke, &c.; to find them seventeen ordinary loaves, and seven inferior loaves, eight gallons of better beer, and 3*d.* per week ; and yearly ten large stock-fish, one bushel of oatmeal, one of rye, two gallons of oil for lamps, one pound of tallow for candles, six loads of turf, and one load of faggots ; also to repair their habitations ; and to find a chaplain to say mass in the chapel of these recluses daily ; their successors to be nominated by the duke and his heirs.   On July 6, 15th Henry VI., the king nominated Isole de Heton, widow, to be an *anachorita* for life, *in loco ad hoc ordinato juxta ecclesiam parochialem de Whalley.*   Isole, however, grew tired of the solitary life, and quitted it ; for afterwards a representation was made to the king that ' divers that had been anchores and recluses in the seyd place aforetyme, have broken oute of the seyd place wherein they were reclusyd, and departyd therefrom wythout any reconsilyation ;' and that Isole de Heton had broken out two years before, and was not willing to return ; and that divers of the women that had been servants there had been with child.   So Henry VI. dissolved the hermitage, and appointed instead two chaplains to say mass daily, &c."   Whittaker thinks that the hermitage occupied the site of some cottages on the west side of the church-

---

* In the " Ancren Riewle," p. 129, we read, " Who can with more facility commit sin than the false recluse ? "

yard, which opened into the churchyard until he had the doors walled up.

There was a similar hermitage for several female recluses in the churchyard of St. Romauld, Shrewsbury, as we learn from a document among the Bishop of Lichfield's registers,* in which he directs the Dean of St. Chadd, or his procurator, to enclose Isolda de Hungerford an anchorite in the houses of the churchyard of St. Romauld, where the other anchorites dwell. Also in the same registry there is a precept, dated Feb. 1, 1310, from Walter de Langton, Bishop, to Emma Sprenghose, admitting her an anchorite in the houses of the churchyard of St. George's Chapel, Salop, and he appoints the archdeacon to enclose her. Another license from Roger, Bishop of Lichfield, dated 1362, to Robert de Worthin, permitting him, on the nomination of Queen Isabella, to serve God in the reclusorium built adjoining (*juxta*) the chapel of St. John Baptist in the city of Coventry, has been published *in extenso* by Dugdale, and we transcribe it for the benefit of the curious.† Thomas Hearne has printed an Episcopal Commission, dated 1402, for enclosing John Cherde, a monk of Ford Abbey. Burnett's " History of Bristol " mentions a commission opened by Bishop William of Wykham, in August, 1403, for enclosing Lucy de Newchurch, an anchoritess in the hermitage of St. Brendon in Bristol. Richard Francis, an ankret, is spoken of as *inter quatuor parietes pro christi inclusus* in Langtoft's " Chronicle," ij. 625.

---

* Owen and Blakeway's " History of Shrewsbury."

† " Rogerus, &c., delecto in Christo filio Roberto de Worthin, cap. salutem, &c. Precipue devotionis affectum, quem ad serviendum Deo in reclusorio juxta capellam Sancti Joh. Babtiste in civitate Coventriensi constructo, et spretis mundi deliciis et ipsius vagis discurribus contemptis, habere te asseres, propensius intuentes, ac volentes te, consideratione nobilis domine, domine Isabelle Regine Anglie nobis pro te supplicante in hujus laudabili proposito confovere, ut in prefato reclusorio morari possis, et recludi et vitam tuam in eodam ducere in tui laudibus Redemptoris, licentiam tibi quantum in nobis est concedi per presentes, quibus sigillum nostrum duximus apponendum. Dat apud Heywood, 5 Kal. Dec. M.D. A.D. MCCCLXII, et consecrationis nostræ tricessimo sexto."— DUGDALE's *Warwickshire*, 2nd Edit., p. 193.

CHAPTER III.

ANCHORAGES.

UST as in a monastery, though it might be large or small in magnitude, simple or gorgeous in style, with more or fewer offices and appendages, according to the number and wealth of the establishment, yet there was always a certain suite of conventual buildings, church, chapter refectory, dormitory, &c., arranged in a certain order, which formed the cloister; and this cloister was the nucleus of all the rest of the buildings of the establishment; so, in a reclusorium, or anchorhold, there was always a "cell" of a certain construction, to which all things else, parlours or chapels, apartments for servants and guests, yards and gardens, were accidental appendages. Bader's rule for recluses in Bavaria* describes the dimensions and plan of the cell minutely; the *domus inclusi* was to be 12 feet long by as many broad, and was to have three windows—one towards the choir (of the church to which it was attached), through which he might receive the Holy Sacrament; another on the opposite side, through which he might receive his victuals; and a third to give light, which last ought always to be closed with glass or horn.

The reader will have already gathered from the preceding extracts that the reclusorium was sometimes a house of timber or stone within the churchyard, and most usually adjoining the church itself. At the west end of Laindon Church, Essex, there is a unique erection of timber, of which we here give a representation. It has been modernised in appearance by

---

* Fosbroke's "British Monachism," p. 372.

the insertion of windows and doors ; and there are no architectural details of a character to reveal with certainty its date, but in its mode of construction—the massive timbers being placed close together—and in its general appearance, there is an air of considerable antiquity. It is improbable that a house would be erected in such a situation after the Reformation, and it accords generally with the descriptions of a recluse house. Probably, however, many of the anchorholds attached to churches were of smaller dimensions ; sometimes, perhaps, only a single little timber

Laindon Church, Essex.

apartment on the ground floor, or sometimes probably raised upon an under croft, according to a common custom in mediæval domestic buildings. Very probably some of those little windows which occur in many of our churches, in various situations, at various heights, and which, under the name of "low side windows," have formed the subject of so much discussion among ecclesiologists, may have been the windows of such anchorholds. The peculiarity of these windows is that they are sometimes merely a square opening, which originally was not glazed, but closed with a shutter; sometimes a small glazed window, in a position where it was clearly not intended to light the church generally; sometimes a window has a stone transom across, and the upper part is glazed, while the lower part is closed only by a shutter. It is clear that some of these may have served to enable the anchorite, living in a cell *outside* the church, to see the altar. It seems to have been such a window which is alluded to in the following incident from Mallory's " Prince Arthur :"—" Then Sir Launcelot armed him and took his horse, and as he rode that way he saw a chapel where was a recluse, which had a window that she might see

Reclusorium, or Anchorhold, at Rettenden, Essex.

up to the altar ; and all aloud she called Sir Launcelot, because he seemed a knight arrant. . . . . . And (after a long conversation) she commanded Launcelot to dinner." In the late thirteenth-century MS., Royal 10 E. IV. at f. 181, is a representation of a recluse-house, in which, besides two two-light arched windows high up in the wall, there is a smaller square " low side window " very distinctly shown. Others of these low side windows may have been for the use of wooden anchorholds built *within* the church, combining two of the usual three windows of the cell, viz., the one to give light, and the one through which to receive food and communicate with the outer world. There is an anchorhold still remaining in a tolerably unmutilated state at Rettenden, Essex. It is a stone building of fifteenth-century date, of two stories, adjoining the north side of the chancel. It is entered by a rather elaborately moulded doorway from the chancel. The lower story is now used as a vestry, and is lighted by a modern window broken through its east wall; but it is described as having been a dark room, and there is no trace of any original window. In the north wall, and towards the east, is a bracket, such as would hold a small statue or a lamp. In the west side of this room, on the left immediately on entering it from the chancel, is the door of a stone winding stair (built up in the nave aisle, but now screened towards the aisle by a very large monument), which gives access to the upper story. This story consists of a room which very exactly agrees with the description of a recluse's cell (see opposite wood-cut). On the south side are two arched niches, in which are stone benches, and the back of the easternmost of these niches is pierced by a small arched window, now blocked up, which looked down upon the altar. On the north side is a chimney, now filled with a modern fireplace, but the chimney is a part of the original building; and westward of the chimney is a small square opening, now filled with modern glazing, but the hook upon which the original shutter hung still remains. This window is not splayed in the usual mediæval manner, but is recessed in such a way as to allow the head of a person to look out, and especially down, with facility. On the exterior this window is about 10 feet from the ground. In this respect it resembles the situation of a low side window in Prior Crawden's Chapel, Ely Cathedral,* which is on the first floor, having a room, lighted only by narrow slits, beneath it; and at the Sainte Chapelle, in Paris, which also has an undercroft, there is a similar example of a side window, at a still greater height from the ground. The east side of the Rettenden reclusorium has now a modern window, probably occupying the place of the original window which gave light to the cell. The stair-turret at the top of the winding staircase, seems to have been intended to serve

---

* Engraved in the *Archæological Journal*, iv. p. 320.

for a little closet : it obtained some light through a small loop which looked out into the north aisle of the church ; the wall on the north side of it is recessed so as to form a shelf, and a square slab of stone, which looks like a portion of a thirteenth-century coffin-stone, is laid upon the top of the newel, and fitted into the wall, so as to form another shelf or little table.

At East Horndon Church, Essex, there are two transept-like projections from the nave. In the one on the south there is a monumental niche in the south wall, upon the back of which are the indents of the brasses of a man and wife and several children ; and there is a tradition, with which these indents are altogether inconsistent, that the heart of the unfortunate Queen Anne Bullen is interred therein. Over this is a chamber, open to the nave, and now used as a gallery, approached by a modern wooden stair ; and there is a projection outside which looks like a chimney, carried out from this floor upwards. The transeptal projection on the north side is very similar in plan. On the ground floor there is a wide, shallow, cinque-foil headed niche (partly blocked) in the east wall ; and there is a wainscot ceiling, very neatly divided into rectangular panels by moulded ribs of the date of about Henry VIII. The existence of the chamber above was unknown until the present rector discovered a door-way in the east wall of the ground floor, which, on being opened, gave access to a stone staircase behind the east wall, which led up into a first-floor chamber, about 12 feet from east to west, and 8 feet from north to south : the birds had had access to it through an unglazed window in the north wall for an unknown period, and it was half filled with their nests ; the floor planks were quite decayed. There is no trace of a chimney here. It is now opened out to the nave to form a gallery. Though we do not find in these two first-floor chambers the arrangements which could satisfy us that they were recluse cells, yet it is very probable that they were habitable chambers, inhabited, if not by recluses, perhaps by chantry priests, serving chantry chapels of the Tyrrells.

Mr. M. H. Bloxam, in an interesting paper in the Transactions of the Lincoln Diocesan Architectural Society, mentions several other anchor-holds :—" Adjoining the little mountain church of S. Patricio, about five miles from Crickhowel, South Wales, is an attached building or cell. It contains on the east side a stone altar, above which is a small window, now blocked up, which looked towards the altar of the church ; but there was no other internal communication between this cell and the church, to the west end of which it is annexed ; it appears as if destined for a recluse who was also a priest." Mr. Bloxam mentions some other examples, very much resembling the one described at Rettenden. The north transept of Clifton Campville Church, Staffordshire, a structure of the fourteenth century, is vaulted and groined with stone ; it measures 17 feet from north to south, and 12 feet from east to west. Over this is a loft or chamber, apparently an anchorhold or *domus inclusi*, access to which is obtained by means of a newell staircase in the south-east angle, from a doorway at the north-east angle of the chancel. A small window on the south side of this chamber, now blocked up, afforded a view into the interior of the church. The roof of this chamber has been lowered, and all the windows blocked up.

" On the north side of the chancel of Chipping Norton Church, Oxford-shire, is a revestry which still contains an ancient stone altar, with its appurtenances, viz., a piscina in the wall on the north side, and a bracket for an image projecting from the east wall, north of the altar. Over this revestry is a loft or chamber, to which access is obtained by means of a staircase in the north-west angle. Apertures in the wall enabled the recluse, probably a priest, here dwelling, to overlook the chancel and north aisle of the church.

" Adjoining the north side of the chancel of Warmington Church, War-wickshire, is a revestry, entered through an ogee-headed doorway in the north wall of the chancel, down a descent of three steps. This revestry contains an ancient stone altar, projecting from a square-headed window in the east wall, and near the altar, in the same wall, is a piscina. In the south-west angle of this revestry is a flight of stone steps, leading up to a chamber or loft. This chamber contains, in the west wall, a fire-place, in the north-west angle a retiring-closet, or jakes, and in the south wall a small pointed window, of decorated character, through which the high-altar in the chancel might be viewed. In the north wall there appears to have been a pointed window, filled with decorated tracery, and in the east wall is another decorated window. This is one of the most interesting and complete specimens of the *domus inclusi* I have met with."*

The chamber which is so frequently found over the porch of our churches, often with a fireplace, and sometimes with a closet within it, may probably have sometimes been inhabited by a recluse. Chambers are also sometimes found in the towers of churches.† Mr. Bloxam mentions a room, with a fire-place, in the tower of Upton Church, Nottinghamshire. Again, at Boyton Church, Wiltshire, the tower is on the north side of the church, "and adjoining the tower on the west side, and communicating with it, is a room which appears to have been once permanently inhabited, and in the north-east angle of this room is a fire-place." At Newport, Salop, the first floor of the tower seems to have been a habitable chamber, and has a little inner chamber corbelled out at the north-west angle of the tower.

We have already hinted that it is not improbable that timber anchor-holds were sometimes erected inside our churches. Or perhaps the recluse lived in the church itself, or, more definitely, in a par-closed chantry chapel, without any chamber being purposely built for him. The indications which lead us to this supposition are these : there is sometimes an ordinary domestic fire-place to be found inside the church. For instance, in the north aisle of Layer Marney Church, Essex, the western part of the aisle is screened off for the chantry of Lord Marney, whose tomb has the chantry altar still remaining, set crosswise at the west end of the tomb; in the eastern division of the aisle there is an ordinary domestic fire-place in the north wall. There is a similar fire-place, of about the same date, in Sir Thomas Bullen's church of Hever, in Kent.

Again, we sometimes find beside the low side-windows already spoken of, an arrangement which shows that it was intended for some one

---

* Reports of the Lincoln Diocesan Archæological Society for 1853, pp. 359-60.

† Peter, Abbot of Clugny, tells us of a monk and priest of that abbey who had for a cell an oratory in a very high and remote steeple-tower, consecrated to the honour of St. Michael the archangel. "Here, devoting himself to divine meditation night and day, he mourned high above mortal things, and seemed with the angels to be present at the nearer vision of his Maker."

habitually to sit there. Thus, at Somerton, Oxfordshire, on the north side of the chancel, is a long and narrow window, with decorated tracery in the head; the lower part is divided by a thick transom, and does not appear to have been glazed. In the interior the wall is recessed beside the window, with a sort of shoulder, exactly adapted to give room for a seat, in such a position that its occupant would get the full benefit of the light through the glazed upper part of the little window, and would be in a convenient position for conversing through the unglazed lower portion of it.

At Elsfield Church, Oxfordshire, there is an early English lancet window, similarly divided by a transom, the lower part, now blocked up, having been originally un-glazed, and the sill of the window in the interior has been formed into a stone seat and desk. We reproduce here a view of the latter from the "Oxford Architectural Society's Guide to the Neighbourhood of Oxford." Perhaps in such instances as these, the recluse may have been a priest serving a chantry altar, and licensed, perhaps, to hear confessions,* for which the seat beside the little open window would be a convenient arrangement.

Window, Elsfield Church.

Lord Scrope's will has already told us of a chaplain dwelling continu-ally (*commoranti continuo*) in the Church of St. Nicholas, Gloucester, and of an anchorite living in the parish church of Stamford. There is a low side-window at Mawgan Church, Cornwall. In the south-east angle between the south transept and the chancel, the inner angle at the junction of the transept and chancel walls is cut away, from the floor upwards, to the

---

In the Lichfield Registers we find that, on February 10, 1409, the bishop granted to Brother Richard Goldestone, late canon of Wombrugge, now recluse at Prior's Lee, near Shiffenale, license to hear confessions. (History of Whalley, p. 55.)

height of six feet, and laterally about five feet in south and east directions from the angle. A short octagonal pillar, six feet high, supports all that remains of the angle of these walls, whilst the walls themselves rest on two flat segmental arches of three feet span. A low diagonal wall is built across the angle thus exposed, and a small lean-to roof is run up from it into the external angle enclosing a triangular space within. In this wall the low side-window is inserted. The sill of the window is four feet from the pavement. Further eastward a priest's door seems to have formed part of the arrangement. The west jamb of the doorway is cut away so that from this triangular space and from the transept beyond a view is obtained of the east window.

The position of the low side-windows at Grade, Cury, and Landewednack is the same as that of Mawgan, but the window itself is different in form, those at Grade and at Cury being small oblong openings, the former 1 ft. 9 in. by 1 ft. 4 in., the sill only 1 ft. 9 in. from the ground; the latter is 1 ft. by 11 in., the sill 3 ft. 4 in. from ground. At Landewednack the window has two lights, square headed, 2 ft. 6 in. by 1 ft. 4 in., sill 4 ft. 3½ in. from ground. A large block of serpentine rock is fixed in the ground beneath the window in a position convenient for a person standing but not kneeling at the window.*

Knighton gives us some particulars of a recluse priest who lived at Leicester. "There was," he says, "in those days at Leicester, a certain priest, hight William of Swynderby, whom they commonly called William the Hermit, because, for a long time, he had lived the hermitical life there; they received him into a certain chamber within the church, because of the holiness they believed to be in him, and they procured for him victuals and a pension, after the manner of other priests." †

In the "Test. Ebor.," p. 244, we find a testator leaving "to the chantry chapel of Kenby my red vestment, ... also the great missal and the great portifer, which I bought of Dominus Thomas Cope, priest and anchorite in that chapel." Blomfield also (ii. 75) tells us of a hermit, who

---

* Paper by J. J. Rogers, *Archæological Journal*, xi. 33.
† Twysden's "Henry de Knighton," vol. ii. p. 2665.

lived in St. Cuthbert's Church, Thetford, and performed divine service therein.

Who has not, at some time, been deeply impressed by the solemn stillness, the holy calm, of an empty church? Earthly passions, and cares, and ambitions, seemed to have died away; one's soul was filled with a spiritual peace. One stood and listened to the wind surging against the walls outside, as the waves of the sea may beat against the walls of an ingulfed temple; and one felt as effectually secluded from the surge and roar of the worldly life outside the sacred walls, as if in such a temple at the bottom of the sea. One gazed upon the monu·mental effigies, with their hands clasped in an endless prayer, and their passionless marble faces turned for ages heavenward, and read their mouldering epitaphs, and moralized on the royal preacher's text—" All is vanity and vexation of spirit." And then one felt the disposition—and, perhaps, indulged it—to kneel before the altar, all alone with God, in that still and solemn church, and pour out one's high-wrought thoughts before Him. At such times one has probably tasted something of the transcendental charm of the life of a recluse priest. One could not sustain the tension long. Perhaps the old recluse, with his experience and his aids, could maintain it for a longer period. But to him, too, the natural reaction must have come in time; and then he had his mechanical occupations to fall back upon—trimming the lamps before the shrines, copying his manuscript, or illuminating its initial letters; perhaps, for health's sake, he took a daily walk up and down the aisle of the church, whose walls re-echoed his measured footfalls; then he had his oft-recurring "hours" to sing, and his books to read; and, to prevent the long hours which were still left him in his little par-closed chapel from growing too wearily monotonous, there came, now and then, a tap at the shutter of his "parlour" window, which heralded the visit of some poor soul, seeking counsel or comfort in his difficulties of this world or the next, or some pilgrim bringing news of distant lands, or some errant knight seeking news of adventures, or some parishioner come honestly to have a dish of gossip with the holy man, about the good and evil doings of his neighbours.

There is a pathetic anecdote in Blomfield's " Norfolk," which will show that the spirit and tl.e tradition of the old recluse priests survived the Reformation. The Rev. Mr. John Gibbs, formerly rector of Gessing, in that county, was ejected from his rectory in 1690 as a non-juror. "He was an odd but harmless man, both in life and conversation. After his ejection he dwelt in the north porch chamber, and laid on the stairs that led up to the rood-loft, between the church and chancel, having a window at his head, so that he could lie in his couch, and see the altar. He lived to be very old, and was buried at Frenze."

Let us turn again to the female recluse, in her anchor-house outside the church. How was her cell furnished? It had always a little altar at the east end, before which the recluse paid her frequent devotions, hearing, besides, the daily mass in church through her window, and receiving the Holy Sacrament at stated times. Bishop Poore advises his recluses to receive it only fifteen times a year. The little square unglazed window was closed with a shutter, and a black curtain with a white cross upon it also hung before the opening, through which the recluse could converse without being seen. The walls appear to have been sometimes painted —of course with devotional subjects. To complete the scene add a comfortable carved oak chair, and a little table, an embroidery frame, and such like appliances for needlework; a book of prayers, and another of saintly legends, not forgetting Bishop Poore's "Ancren Riewle;" a fire on the hearth in cold weather, and the cat, which Bishop Poore expressly allows, purring beside it; and lastly paint in the recluse, in her black habit and veil, seated in her chair; or prostrate before her little altar; or on her knees beside her church window listening to the chanted mass; or receiving her basket of food from her servant, through the open parlour window; or standing before its black curtain, conversing with a stray knight-errant; or putting her white hand through it, to give an alms to some village crone or wandering beggar.

A few extracts from Bishop Poore's "Ancren Riewle," already several times alluded to, will give life to the picture we have painted. Though intended for the general use of recluses, it seems to have been specially addressed, in the first instance, to three sisters, who, in the bloom of youth, forsook the world, and became the tenants of a reclusorium. It would seem that in such cases each recluse had a separate cell, and did not communicate, except on rare occasions, with her fellow inmates ; and each had her own separate servant to wait upon her. Here are some particulars as to their communication with the outer world. " Hold no conversation with any man out of a church window, but respect it for the sake of the Holy Sacrament which ye see there through ;* and at other times (other whiles) take your women to the window of the house (huses thurle), other men and women to the parlour-window to speak when necessary ; nor ought ye (to converse) but at these two windows." Here we have three windows ; we have no difficulty in understanding which was the church-window, and the parlour-window—the window *pour parler ;* but what was the house-window, through which the recluse might speak to her servant ? Was it merely the third glazed window, through which she might, if it were convenient, talk with her maid, but not with strangers, because she would be seen through it ? or was it a window in the larger anchorholds, between the recluse cell, and the other apartment in which her maid lived, and in which, perhaps, guests were entertained ? The latter seems the more probable explanation, and will receive further confirmation when we come to the directions about the entertainment of guests. The recluse was not to give way to the very natural temptation to put her head out of the open window, to get sometimes a wider view of the world about her. " A peering anchoress, who is always thrusting her head outward," he compares to " an untamed bird in a cage "—poor human bird ! In another place he gives a more serious exhortation on the same subject. " Is not she too forward and foolhardy who holds her head boldly forth on the open battlements while men with crossbow bolts without assail the castle ? Surely our foe, the warrior of hell, shoots, as I ween, more bolts at one anchoress than at seventy and seven secular ladies. The battlements of the castle are the windows of their houses ; let her not look out at them, lest she

---

* The translator of this book for the Camden Society's edition of it, says " therein," but the word in the original Saxon English is " ther thurgh." It refers to the window looking into the church, through which the recluse looked down daily upon the celebration of the mass.

have the devil's bolts between her eyes before she even thinks of it." Here are directions how to carry on her "parlements":—"First of all, when you have to go to your parlour-window, learn from your maid who it is that is come ; . . . . . and when you must needs go forth, go forth in the fear of God to a priest, ... and sit and listen, and not cackle." They were to be on their guard even with religious men, and not even confess, except in presence of a witness. " If any man requests to see you (*i.e.* to have the black curtain drawn aside), ask him what good might come of it. . . . If any one become so mad and unreasonable that he puts forth his hand toward the window-cloth (curtain), shut the window (*i.e.* close the shutter) quickly, and leave him ; . . . . and as soon as any man falls into evil discourse, close the window, and go away with this verse, that he may hear it, ' The wicked have told me foolish tales, but not according to thy law ; ' and go forth before your altar, and say the ' Miserere.' " Again, " Keep your hands within your windows, for handling or touching between a man and an anchoress is a thing unnatural, shameful, wicked," &c.

The bishop adds a characteristic piece of detail to our picture when he speaks of the fair complexions of the recluses because not sunburnt, and their white hands through not working, both set in strong relief by the black colour of the habit and veil. He says, indeed, that " since no man seeth you, nor ye see any man, ye may be content with your clothes white or black." But in practice they seem usually to have worn black habits, unless, when attached to the church of any monastery, they may have worn the habit of the order. They were not to wear rings, brooches, ornamented girdles, or gloves. " An anchoress," he says, " ought to take sparingly (of alms), only that which is necessary (*i.e.* she ought not to take alms to give away again). If she can spare any fragments of her food, let her send them away (to some poor person) privately out of her dwelling. For the devil," he says elsewhere, " tempts anchoresses, through their charity, to collect to give to the poor, then to a friend, then to make a feast." " There are anchoresses," he says, " who make their meals with their friends without ; that is too much friendship." The editor thinks this to mean that some anchoresses left their cells, and went to dine at the houses of their friends ; but the word is *gistes* (guests), and, more probably,

it only means that the recluse ate her dinner in her cell while a guest ate hers in the guest-room of the reclusorium, with an open window between, so that they could see and converse with one another. For we find in another place that she was to maintain " silence always at meals ; . . . . . and if any one hath a guest whom she holds dear, she may cause her maid, as in her stead, to entertain her friend with glad cheer, and she shall have leave to open her window once or twice, and make signs to her of gladness." But " let no *man* eat in your presence, except he be in great need. The narrative already given at p. 109, of the visit of St. Richard the hermit to Dame Margaret the recluse of Anderby, also shows that in exceptional cases a recluse ate with men. The incident of the head of the recluse, in her convulsive sleep, falling at the window at which the hermit was reclining, and leaning partly upon him,* is explained by the theory that they were sitting in separate apartments, each close by this house window, which was open between them. As we have already seen, in the case of Sir Percival, a man might even sleep in the reclusorium ; and so the Rule says, " let no man sleep within your walls " as a general rule ; " if, however, great necessity should cause your house to be used " by travellers, " see that ye have a woman of unspotted life with you day and night."

As to their occupations, he advises them to make " no purses and blod-bendes of silk, but shape and sew and mend church vestments, and poor people's clothes, and help to clothe yourselves and your domestics." " An anchoress must not become a school-mistress, nor turn her house into a school for children. Her maiden may, however, teach any little girl concerning whom it might be doubtful whether she should learn among the boys."†

Doubtless, we are right in inferring from the bishop's advice not to do certain things, that anchoresses were in the habit of doing them. From this kind of evidence we glean still further traits. He suggests to them that in confession they will perhaps have to mention such faults as these,

---

* " Caput suum decidit ad fenestram ad quam se reclinabit sanctus Dei Ricardus."

† In one of the stories of Reginald of Durham we learn that a school, according to a custom then " common enough," was kept in the church of Norham on Tweed, the parish priest being the teacher. (Wright's " Domestic Manners of the Middle Ages," p. 117.)

"I played or spoke thus in the church; went to the play in the church-yard;* looked on at this, or at the wrestling, or other foolish sports; spoke thus, or played, in the presence of secular men, or of religious men, in a house of anchorites, and at a different window than I ought; or, being alone in the church, I thought thus." Again he mentions, "Sitting too long at the parlour-window, spilling ale, dropping crumbs." Again we find, "Make no banquetings, nor encourage any strange vagabonds about the gate." But of all their failings, gossiping seems to have been the besetting sin of anchoresses. "People say of anchoresses that almost every one hath an old woman to feed her ears, a prating gossip, who tells her all the tales of the land, a magpie that chatters to her of everything that she sees or hears; so that it is a common saying, from mill and from market, from smithy and from anchor-house, men bring tidings."

Let us add the sketch drawn of them by the unfavourable hand of Bilney the Reformer, in his "Reliques of Rome," published in 1563, and we have done :—"As touching the monastical sect of recluses, and such as be shutte up within walls, there unto death continuall to remayne, giving themselves to the mortification of carnal effects, to the contemplation of heavenly and spirituall thinges, to abstinence, to prayer, and to such other ghostly exercises, as men dead to the world, and havyng their lyfe hidden with Christ, I have not to write. Forasmuch as I cannot fynde probably in any author whence the profession of anckers and anckresses had the beginning and foundation, although in this behalf I have talked with men of that profession which could very little or nothing say of the matter. Notwithstanding, as the Whyte Fryers father that order on Helias the prophet (but falsely), so likewise do the ankers and ankresses make that holy and virtuous matrone Judith their patroness and foundress; but how unaptly who seeth not? Their profession and religion differeth as far

---

* These two expressions seem to imply that recluses sometimes went out of their cell, not only into the church, but also into the churchyard. We have already noticed that the technical word "cell" seems to have included everything within the enclosure wall of the whole establishment. Is it possible that in the case of anchorages adjoining churches, the churchyard wall represented this enclosure, and the "cell" included both church and churchyard?

from the manners of Judith as light from darknesse, or God from the devill, as shall manifestly appere to them that will diligentlye conferre the history of Judith with their life and conversation. Judith made herself a privy chamber where she dwelt (sayth the scripture), being closed in with her maydens. Our recluses also close themselves within the walls, but they suffer no man to be there with them. Judith ware a smoche of heare, but our recluses are both softly and finely apparalled. Judith fasted all the days of her lyfe, few excepted. Our recluses eate and drinke at all tymes of the beste, being of the number of them *qui curios simulant et Bacchanalia vivunt.* Judith was a woman of a very good report. Our recluses are reported to be superstitious and idolatrous persons, and such as all good men flye their company. Judith feared the Lord greatly, and lyved according to His holy word. Our recluses fear the pope, and gladly doe what his pleasure is to command them. Judith lyved of her own substance and goods, putting no man to charge. Our recluses, as persons only borne to consume the good fruits of the erth, lyve idely of the labour of other men's handes. Judith, when tyme required, came out of her closet, to do good unto other. Our recluses never come out of their lobbies, sincke or swimme the people. Judith put herself in jeopardy for to do good to the common countrye. Our recluses are unprofitable clods of the earth, doing good to no man. Who seeth not how farre our ankers and ankresses differe from the manners and life of this vertuous and godly woman Judith, so that they cannot justly claime her to be their patronesse? Of some idle and superstitious heremite borrowed they their idle and superstitious religion. For who knoweth not that our recluses have grates of yron in theyr spelunckes, and dennes out of the which they looke, as owles out of an yvye todde, when they will vouchsafe to speake with any man at whose hand they hope for advantage? So reade we in 'Vitis Patrum,' that John the Heremite so enclosed himself in his hermitage that no person came in unto him; to them that came to visite him he spoke through a window onely. Our ankers and ankresses professe nothing but a solitary lyfe in their hallowed house, wherein they are inclosed wyth the vowe of obedience to the pope, and to their ordinary bishop. Their apparel is indifferent, so it be dissonant from the laity. No kind of meates they are forbidden to eat. At midnight they are bound to say certain prayers. Their profession is counted to be among other professions so hardye and so streight that they may by no means be suffered to come out of their houses except it be to take on them an harder and streighter, which is to be made a bishop."

It is not to be expected that mediæval paintings should give illustrations of persons who were thus never visible in the world. In the pictures of the hermits of the Egyptian desert, on the walls of the Campo Santo at Pisa, we see a representation of St. Anthony holding a conversation with St. John the Hermit, who is just visible through his grated window, "like an owl in an ivy tod," as Bilney says ; and we have already given a picture of Sir Percival knocking at the door of a female recluse. Bilney says, that they wore any costume, "so it were dissonant from the laity;" but in all probability they commonly wore a costume similar in colour to that of the male hermits. The picture which we here give of an anchoress, is taken from a figure of St. Paula, one of the anchorite saints of the desert, in the same picture of St. Jerome, which has already supplied us, in the figure of St. Damasus, with our best picture of the hermit's costume.

St. Paula.

The service for enclosing a recluse * may be found in some of the old Service Books. We derive the following account of it from an old black-letter *Manuale ad usum percelebris ecclesie Sarisburiensis* (London, 1554), in the British Museum. The rubric before the service orders that no

---

* A commission given by William of Wykham, Bishop of Winchester, for enclosing Lucy de Newchurch as an anchoritess in the hermitage of St. Brendun, at Bristol, is given in Burnett's "History and Antiquities of Bristol," p. 61.

one shall be enclosed without the bishop's leave; that the candidate shall be closely questioned as to his motives; that he shall be taught not to entertain proud thoughts, as if he merited to be set apart from intercourse with common men, but rather on account of his own infirmity it was good that he should be removed from contact with others, that he might be kept out of sin himself, and not contaminate them. So that the recluse should esteem himself to be condemned for his sins, and shut up in his solitary cell as in a prison, and unworthy, for his sins, of the society of men. There is a note, that this office shall serve for both sexes. On the day before the ceremony of inclusion, the *Includendus*—the person about to be inclosed—was to confess, and to fast that day on bread and water; and all that night he was to watch and pray, having his wax taper burning, in the monastery,* near his inclusorium. On the morrow, all being assembled in church, the bishop, or priest appointed by him, first addressed an exhortation to the people who had come to see the ceremony, and to the includendus himself, and then began the service with a response, and several appropriate psalms and collects. After that, the priest put on his chasuble, and began mass, a special prayer being introduced for the includendus. After the reading of the gospel, the includendus stood before the altar, and offered his taper, which was to remain burning on the altar throughout the mass; and then, standing before the altar-step, he read his profession, or if he were a layman (and unable to read), one of the chorister boys read it for him. And this was the form of his profession :—" I, brother (or sister) N, offer and present myself to serve the Divine Goodness in the order of Anchorites, and I promise to remain, according to the rule of that order, in the service of God, from henceforth, by the grace of God, and the counsel of the Church." Then he signed the document in which his profession was written with the sign of the cross, and laid it upon the altar on bended knees. Then the bishop or priest said a prayer, and asperged with holy water the habit of the includendus; and he put on the habit, and prostrated himself before the altar, and so remained, while the

---

* " In monasterio inclusorio suo vicino; " it seems as if the writer of the rubric were specially thinking of the inclusoria within monasteries.

priest and choir sang over him the hymn *Veni Creator Spiritus*, and then proceeded with the mass.   First the priest communicated, then the includendus, and then the rest of the congregation ; and the mass was concluded. Next his wax taper, which had all this time been burning on the altar, was given to the includendus, and a procession was formed ; first the choir ; then the includendus, clad in his proper habit, and carrying his lighted taper ; then the bishop or priest, in his mass robes ; and then the people following ; and so they proceeded, singing a solemn litany, to the cell.   And first the priest entered alone into the cell, and asperged it with holy water, saying appropriate sentences ; then he consecrated and blessed the cell, with prayers offered before the altar of its chapel.   The third of these short prayers may be transcribed : " Benedic domine domum istam et locum istum, ut sit in eo sanitas, sanctitas, castitas, virtus, victoria, sanctimonia, humilitas, lenitas, mansuetudo, plenitudo, legis et obedientæ Deo Patre et Filio et Spiritui Sancto et sit super locum istum et super omnes habitantes in eo tua larga benedictio, ut in his manufactis habitaculis cum solemtate manentes ipsi tuum sit semper habitaculum.   Per dominum," &c.   Then the bishop or priest came out, and led in the includendus, still carrying his lighted taper, and solemnly blessed him.   And then—a mere change in the tense of the rubric has an effect which is quite pathetic ; it is no longer the *includendus*, the person to be enclosed, but the *inclusus*, the enclosed one, he or she upon whom the doors of the cell have closed for ever in this life—then the enclosed is to maintain total and solemn silence throughout, while the doors are securely closed, the choir chanting appropriate psalms.   Then the celebrant causes all the people to pray for the inclusus privately, in solemn silence, to God, for whose love he has left the world, and caused himself to be inclosed in that strait prison.   And after some concluding prayers, the procession left the inclusus to his solitary life, and returned, chanting, to the church, finishing at the step of the choir.

One cannot read this solemn—albeit superstitious—service, in the quaint old mediæval character, out of the very book which has, perhaps, been used in the actual enclosing of some recluse, without being moved.   Was it some frail woman, with all the affections of her heart and the hopes of her earthly life shattered, who sought the refuge of this living tomb ? was it some man of strong passions, wild and fierce in his crimes, as wild and fierce in his penitence? or was it some enthusiast, with the over-excited religious sensibility, of which we have instances enough in these days? We can see them still, in imagination, prostrate, " in total and solemn silence," before the wax taper placed upon the altar of the little chapel, and listening while the chant of the returning procession grows fainter and fainter in the distance. Ah ! we may scornfully smile at it all as a wild super-stition, or treat it coldly as a question of mere antiquarian interest ; but what broken hearts, what burning passions, have been shrouded under that recluse's robe, and what wild cries of human agony have been stifled under that " total and solemn silence ! " When the processional chant had died away in the distance, and the recluse's taper had burnt out on his little altar, was that the end of the tragedy, or only the end of the first act? Did the broken heart find repose? Did the wild spirit grow tame? Or did the one pine away and die like a flower in a dungeon, and the other beat itself to death against the bars of its self-made cage?

CHAPTER IV.

CONSECRATED WIDOWS OF THE MIDDLE AGES.

BESIDES all other religious people living under vows, in community in monasteries, or as solitaries in their anchorages, there were also a number of Widows vowed to that life and devoted to the service of God, who lived at home in their own houses or with their families. This was manifestly a continuation, or imitation, of the primitive Order of Widows, of whom St. Paul speaks in his first Epistle to Timothy (ch. v.). For although religious women, from an early period (fourth century), were usually nuns, the primitive Orders of Deaconesses and Widows did not altogether cease to exist in the Church. The Service Books * contain offices for their benediction; and though it is probable that in fact a deaconess was very rarely consecrated in the Western Church, yet the number of allusions to widows throughout the Middle Ages leads us to suspect that there may have been no inconsiderable number of them. A common form of commission† to a suffragan bishop includes the consecrating of widows. From the Pontifical of Edmund Lacey, Bishop of Exeter, of the fourteenth century, we give a sketch of the service.‡ It is the same in substance as those in the earlier books. First, a rubric states that though a widow may be blessed on any day, it is more fitting that she be blessed on a holy day, and especially on the Lord's day. Between the

---

* The Ordo Romanus. The Pontifical of Egbert. The Pontifical of Bishop Lacey.

† *Guardian* newspaper, Feb. 7, 1870.

‡ Surrey Society's Transactions, vol. iii. p. 218.

Epistle and the Gospel, the bishop sitting on a faldstool facing the people, the widow kneeling before the bishop is to be interrogated if she desires, putting away all carnal affections, to be joined as a spouse to Christ. Then she shall publicly in the vulgar tongue profess herself, in the bishop's hands, resolved to observe perpetual continence. Then the bishop blesses her habit (clamidem), saying a collect. Then the bishop, genuflecting, begins the hymn *Veni Creator Spiritus ;* the widow puts on the habit and veil, and the bishop blesses and gives her the ring ; and with a final prayer for appropriate virtues and blessings, the ordinary service of Holy Communion is resumed, special mention of the widow being made therein.

These collects are of venerable age, and have much beauty of thought and expression. The reader may be glad to see one of them as an example, and as an indication of the spirit in which people entered into these religious vows : " O God, the gracious inhabiter of chaste bodies and lover of uncorrupt souls, look we pray Thee, O Lord, upon this Thy servant, who humbly offers her devotion to Thee. May there be in her, O Lord, the gift of Thy spirit, a prudent modesty, a wise graciousness, a grave gentleness, a chaste freedom ; may she be fervent in charity and love nothing beside Thee (*extra te*) ; may she live praiseworthy and not desire praise ; may she fear Thee and serve Thee with a chaste love ; be Thou to her, O Lord, honour, Thou delight ; be Thou in sorrow her comfort, in doubt her counsellor ; be Thou to her defence in injury, in tribulation patience, in poverty abundance, in fasting food, in sickness medicine. By Thee, whom she desires to love above all things, may she keep what she has vowed ; so that by Thy help she may conquer the old enemy, and cast out the defilements of sin ; that she may be decorated with the gift of fruit sixty fold,* and adorned with the lamps of all virtues, and by Thy grace may be worthy to join the company of the elect widows. This we humbly ask through Jesus Christ our Lord."

* The same collect, with a few variations, was used also in the consecration of nuns. Virgin chastity was held to bring forth fruit a hundred fold ; widowed chastity, sixty fold ; married chastity, thirty fold.

In a paper in the " Surrey Transactions," vol. iii. p. 208, Mr. Baigent, the writer of it, finds two, and only two, entries of the consecration of widows in the Episcopal Registers of Winchester, which go back to the early part of the reign of Edward I.   The first of these is on May 4, 1348, of the Lady Aleanor Giffard, probably, says Mr. Baigent, the widow of John Giffard, of Bowers Giffard, in Essex.   The other entry, on October 18, 1379, is of the Benediction of Isabella Burgh, the widow of a citizen of London (whose will is given by Mr. Baigent), and of Isabella Golafre, widow of Sir John Golafre.

The profession of the widow is given in old French, and a translation of it in old English, as follows : " In ye name of God, Fader and Sone and Holy Ghost.   Iche Isabelle Burghe, that was sometyme wyfe of Thomas Burghe, wyche that is God be taught helpynge the grace of God [the parallel French is, Quest à Dieu commande ottriaunte la grace de Dieu] behote [promise] conversione of myn maners, and make myn avows to God, and to is swete moder Seynte Marie and to alle seintz, into youre handes leve [dear] fader in God, William be ye grace of God Bisshope of Wynchestre, that fro this day forward I schal ben chaste of myn body and in holy chastite kepe me treweliche and devouteliche all ye dayes of myn life." Another form of profession is written on the lower margin of the Exeter Pontifical, and probably in the handwriting of Bishop Lacy : " I, N., wedowe, avowe to God perpetuall chastite of my body from henceforward, and in the presence of the honorable fadyr in God, my Lord N., by the grace of God, Bishop of N., I promyth sabilly to leve in the Church, a wedowe.   And this to do, of myne own hand I subscribe this writing : *Et postea faciat signum crucis.*"

Another example of a widow in the Winchester registers is that of Elizabeth de Julien, widow of John Plantagenet, Earl of Kent, who made that vow to Bishop William de Edyndon, but afterwards married Sir Eustache Dabrichecourt, September 29, 1360, whereupon proceedings were commenced against her by the Archbishop of Canterbury, who imposed on her a severe and life-long penance.   She survived her second husband many years, and dying in 1411, was buried in the choir of the Friars Minor at Winchester, near the tomb of her first husband.

The epitaph on the monumental brass of Joanna Braham, A.D. 1519, at Frenze, in Norfolk, describes her as " Vidua ac Deo devota."

In the Book of the Knight of La Tour-Landry is a description of a lady who, if she had not actually taken the vows of widowhood, lived the life we should suppose to be that of a vowess. " It is of a good lady whiche longe tyme was in wydowhode. She was of a holy lyf, and moste humble and honourable, as the whiche every yere kepte and held a feste upon Crystemasse-day of her neyghbours bothe farre and nere, tyll her halle was ful of them. She served and honoured eche one after his degree, and specially she bare grete reverence to the good and trewe wymmen, and to them whiche has deservyd to be worshipped. Also she was of suche customme that yf she knewe any poure gentyll woman that shold be wedded she arayed her with her jewels. Also she wente to the obsequye of the poure gentyll wymmen, and gaf there torches, and all such other lumynary as it neded thereto. Her dayly ordenaunce was that she rose erly ynough, and had ever freres, and two or three chappellayns whiche sayd matyns before her within her oratorye; and after she herd a hyhe masse and two lowe, and sayd her servyse full devoutely; and atter this she wente and arayed herself, and walked in her gardyn, or else aboute her plase, sayenge her other devocions and prayers. And as tyme was she wente to dyner; and after dyner, if she wyste and knewe ony seke folke or wymmen in theyr childbedde, she went to see and vysited them, and made to be brought to them of her best mete. And then, as she myght not go herself, she had a servant propyer therefore, whiche rode upon a lytell hors, and bare with him grete plente of good mete and drynke for to gyve to the poure and seke folk there as they were. And after she had herd evensonge she went to her souper, yf she fasted not. And tymely she wente to bedde; made her styward to come to her to wete what mete sholde be had the next daye, and lyved by good ordenaunce, and wold be purveyed byfore of alle such thynge that was nedefull for her household. She made grete abstynence, and wered the hayre * upon the Wednesday and upon the Fryday. . . . . And she rose

---

* Hair-cloth garment worn next the skin for mortification.

everye night thre tymes, and kneled downe to the ground by her bedde, and redryd thankynges to God, and prayd for al Crysten soules, and dyd grete almes to the poure. This good lady, that wel is worthy to be named and preysed, had to name my lady Cecyle of Ballavylle. . . . . She was the most good and curtoys lady that ever I knewe or wyste in ony countrey, and that lesse was envious, and never she wold here say ony evyll of no body, but excused them, and prayd to God that they myght amende them, and that none was that knewe what to hym shold happe. . . . . She had a ryhte noble ende, and as I wene ryht agreable to God ; and as men say commonely, of honest and good lyf cometh ever a good ende."

In post-Reformation times there are biographies of holy women which show that the idea of consecrated widowhood was still living in the minds of the people. Probably the dress commonly worn by widows throughout their widowhood is a remnant of the mediæval custom.

This is the end of this publication.

Any remaining blank pages are for our book binding
requirements and are blank on purpose.

To search thousands of interesting publications like this one,
please remember to visit our website at:

http://www.kessinger.net

Printed in the United Kingdom
by Lightning Source UK Ltd.
119800UK00001B/110